Shaun Best, Manuscript: The Best Quest
Challenged Conquistadors, Inc.
1110 Pine Circle
Smackover, AR 71762

Dear Director:

My story, non-fiction, involves the victory involved in dealing with
the cognitive challenges/disabilities (history will speak
unfavorably of our treatment of humans) a three-month coma
(cognitive challenges) at the age of 12 in rural Swift in 1977. I
was recruited by two national foundations one is a national retailer
& the other is concerned about those with brain trauma, which has
increased my cognitive challenges. I or my organization "Challenged
Conquistadors, Inc." is to encourage survivors of traumatic brain
injuries succeed & complete making a college campus comply with the
Americans with Disabilities Act (ADA) of 1990; accessibility. I was
to complete a two year teaching certificate by 1996, while doing
this. The book addresses: how the brain/mind can conquer cognitive
challenges/disabilities & demonstrating recovery for those surviving
individuals that they can succeed. If I'm not wrong, this was the
first President Bush's obligation. My grade point average for my
early education classes was a 3.2 or a B average. This accessible
work took five years to secure 1993-1998, which involved 24
additional cognitive challenges due to the campus being non-
accessible (illegal). The cost of non-accessibility has cost me
many jobs, thus lowering my quality of life with 58 (today 8/16/16)
cognitive challenges. I wonder how many people (veterans) know this
feeling? This college Southern Arkansas University was allowed to
deny me a teaching certificate. I'm finally teaching after 16 years
and would like to provide hope, encouragement, determination,
patience, etc., to those dealing with cognitive injuries, since one
occurs every 18.5 seconds in America and every 15 seconds in Canada.
I've lived that others may see that cognitive challenges may
successfully be dealt with, with the different mental & physical
challenges to secure other life goals. I'm a servant demonstrating
the awesome power of God; through His son Jesus Christ.

My recovery has been slowed because from 1978-2007, recently, I was
on the wrong medications for my brain challenges for many years. As
you can see, I promote myself as challenged (optimistic explanatory
learning style), since 1978, rather than disabled, retarded,
handicapped, etc., (pessimistic explanatory learning style). These
cruel terms are a negative, legal, educational, self-fulfilling
prophecy or a disability environment, which do more harm since
"Self-Matters", Dr. Phil, Ph.D & "The Unschooled Mind", Gardner.
More on the optimistic learning style vs. pessimistic learning style
can be found at the Positive Psychology Center, Dr. Martin EP
Seligman, Ph.D.

One must remember that my mother almost institutionalized me after the accident in 1977, then another attempt by an employer in 1996; then an uncle (fathers side) tried 1997; then another employer tried this again in 1999; then another uncle tried (mothers side) around 2004, but all failed. These attempts by the state could have contributed to my non-acceptance or denial of a teaching certificate from 1993-2006, perhaps intentional discrimination. The improvements with the newest medication ('07-Invega: better moods, patience, reduced outbursts, reduced bitterness, reduced anger; 4.14.08-Excelon: Better Balance, Reduced Depression, Better Memory, Better Coordination.)

I activate, demonstrate, educate, initiate, motivate, stimulate, and validate that brain challenges can be conquered. I believe strongly in Gods' BARS: Believe Achieve Receive Success. Have A Optimistic Day the Best Way: Positivism!! What is positivism? Doing away with the negativity/negativism in the disability environment with beneficial terminology like challenged, differently abled, multiple intelligences, etc., i.e., positivism. We are humans, too.

www.positive-personal.growth.com/challenged-conquistador-inc.html

http://www.youtube.com/watch?v=inmBE1sus90

http://www.educationnews.org/ed_reports/107714.html

The Best Quest / Common Struggles, Uncommon Results

The brain can conquer challenges (history will judge us as inhumanely as we judge others) demonstrating recovery for the surviving veterans that they know, (authoritative proof/convincing evidence) they may succeed.

Thank the you all for your continued assistance with my recovery, I appreciate it & I hope I serve you well?

Shaun Best, Protector of the Natural State, LifeSaver
Challenged Conquistadors, Inc.
1110 Pine Circle
Smackover, AR 71762
(870)725-5119

Preface

I hope my life's story will provide the needed proof so that

others can benefit from their unique cognitively/brain challenged

situation, because it doesn't have to be a negative event, it can

be positive like mine.

I don't think anyone likes to be labeled as disabled,
because this means I accept the definition "to deprive of legal
right, qualification, or capacity". This promotes discredit
ability, which denies us independence. When you are viewed as
brain disabled, people view/treat you as if you are damned,
detrimental, a hindrance, legally negatively, etc. If we truly
desire peace for everyone, then why do we label/limit humans
created by God as disabled, disadvantaged, handicapped, cripple,
retarded, etc.? Where is God/religion? Why would our government
try to confine us with self-limiting/disabling terms? I made
other plans, according to the Heavenly Father. It can be said
that these words are inhumane. These words/terms are disgraceful
& hurtful, which doesn't promote individual success, which is
needed for a successful nation & unity.

Where is the unity that is with the United States?
If we truly trust in God, then why does the US judge humans as
disabled? The Bible state "Judge not, that ye be not judged." in
Matthew 7:1, what example does this set for us? Wouldn't God be
happier with us, if we treated all humans with the respect & the
care He does? I'll bet God doesn't appreciate it when we condemn
His humans or your relatives as disabled? I know from Gods' word
(Bible: King James Version) that we are all created in his own
image, which is not disabled, etc., like many are labeled at
birth, Genesis 1:27: "So God created man in his own image, in the
image of God he him; male & female created he them"; Matthew
Chapter 5, v.11, "Blessed are ye, when men shall revile (to abuse

verbally, i.e., disabled, handicapped, cripple, etc.) you, and persecute you, shall say all manner of evil against you falsely, for my sake". Are we a reviling nation? When one speaks of the potential of the disabled aren't we speaking ill of Gods' creation? How do we want history to remember us?

Some words create different perspectives, which cause separation, so do we really want to alienate anyone with inferior terms? The example I set, is also an attempt to save American's at least $40 trillion dollars over the next 10 years, because these individuals labeled, contradictorily as such will cost you & others to support! I am not out to make anyone angry with me, but a beneficial change for humanity is needed, I feel, before we are to have full participation of all human potential.

Evidence of recovery is the tool needed for others to battle against cognitive challenges, successfully.

First & foremost, Glory be to God, because without him I would not be here! The work that I have done has been for one reason and that is to spread the knowledge that God is foremost, the greatest miracle maker & second, all human potential is great! I hopefully will provide adequate proof of success, authoritative proof.

The following are statements from my doctors, On March 3, '89, "This is to certify that Shaun Best is disabled due to an old brain injury. He is on constant medication for epilepsy., by Dr. Que," "In '92, his ability to retain newly learned information was poor., by Dr. A. Smith, Ph.D., "12/6, '94-In '77, Shaun Best had suffered a significant head injury with three months of coma." "Please note that his seizure-like (but non-epileptic) spells are part & parcel of his pos-traumatic state.": "6/6, '96-Shaun's seizures are of a minor type, he never hurts himself, and he regains awareness within 1-2 minutes. They require no particular intervention and are of a benign (of a gentle disposition: GRACIOUS) {a verbal illustration is a benign teacher} nature.": I find in complimentary that the Webster's Ninth New Collegiate Dictionary '83 uses benign in this manner for its first example. This is the first dictionary that I bought in '83 when I started college at the university I attended in 1983. "May 2, '97-....he has startle attacks....which present no danger to himself or others & followed by quick recovery." "I am very concerned if this basically benign handicap is considered a hindrance to his academic progress.", by Dr. Field. He has been my doctor since '92. On January 18, '00, I and my spouse went to visit him & he told us (orally) that I never had seizures, but what is called absence episodes. From epilepsy/seizures (convulsive attacks both mental & physical) to having positive absence episodes (momentary stares) is a longer journey & think of the number of people who think badly of me & are afraid of me, like employers, needlessly?

First, I would like to state my mission, which is my life, & then begin with my story for clarity. My mission is to save your relative's life, our nation, by reducing the number of cognitive challenges (CC), which could cost us/save more than $40,000,000,000,000 over the next 10 years. How do I get this figure, simple, TBI's occur at 2,000,000 a year according to the 1990 Census multiplied by just an average cost of $2,000,000, then we have spent roughly $40,000,000,000,000 in the '90's.

My plea of conquering this vicious limitation before it destroys our nation is critical. Our ancestors established this nation so that we all might be able & free, Mr. & Mrs. Washington, Mr. & Mrs. Jefferson, Mr. & Mrs. Lincoln, etc. The Cognitively Challenged community is an untapped market which can greatly benefit our nation, if we act correctly. Many opportunities no longer exist to spread the positive message that Cognitive Challenge's may be conquered, since many are forced to wear the brain disabled (meaning not-able or to deprive of legal right, qualification, etc.), disadvantaged (meaning an imposed handicap), crippled (meaning a lame or partly disabled person or animal), damaged (meaning a loss or harm resulting from injury), or handicapped (meaning a disadvantaged imposed) label/terms (verbal abuse), by our national government, needlessly. Where is the compassion, love, honorable, caring, considerate, humane, or correct terminology, since we boast about our God being of love? Shouldn't we show it? I am not condemning our government, that would be foolish, but haven't we learned enough about segregation, rejection, exclusion, divisions, & the difficulties it poses? Hasn't the time come for us to all work together? If you check history, the term handicap originated in England after the war when soldiers came home missing legs, arms, eyes, etc., their government allowed these individuals to solicit funds from street corners since they could not work. The funds were collected by holding their caps from their head in their hands, thus handicap. It would seem that they want us to lie down & not be productive or quit trying to secure our own independence. This is not capitalism for all, which America (free enterprise capital) is based on. Shouldn't we try to leave a beneficial change that will positively influence everyone in the world vs. continued negative abuse/destruction & defamation!

Disabilities are like slavery (submission to a dominating influence) & terrorism (the systematic use of terror esp. as a means of coercion). Terrorism & slavery are both violent & criminal. We cannot change the past; however we can brighten the future for many others that will hopefully open the right door for many more than the door that has been closed on many in history, because of disability. I propose that you wear these labels & then demonstrate positive benefits. Of course do this by yourself, as I have done, while being told that I would never be normal again. I preferred to be called/labeled "challenged," because it offers security & assurance that I am positively accepted without any negative implication like those listed above. History will judge us accordingly! If my absence episodes had been labeled/termed as such, instead of seizures, then perhaps I would have achieved more success in the last 39 years. My degrees were obtained on varying amounts of medication: the first was completed on no medication other than illegal drugs; the second was achieved on varying degrees of incorrect medication & correct medication; & the last attempt was on proper medication, but perhaps, too much at some times, therefore I was denied a teaching degree/certification because of 24 cognitive challenges on a campus that was non-accessible.

Look at how much more the word challenge (positive) appears versus the negative-disable, today, when describing humans as compared to ten years ago. Isn't it great? As the leader of the free world, the dominate nation, we must lead, good conquers evil, right conquers wrong! Negatives cannot be positive. Think about it. Should it be done or what will become of our planet, i.e., Almighty God vs. the devil? I have a new idea: It could have been worse! I challenge all survivors of Cognitive Challenges to do better than I've done, because it is possible! I fight disability, because it is damning my abilities, i.e., "not able"! Case Closed. Many progressive accounts better themselves, however disability can never be improved. Disability was started in the 1930's with President Roosevelt with good intentions. I believe my life has gone the way God desired so that I can be a positive light in the darkness for others with cognitive challenges, because disabilities only diminish potential. Our future is in jeopardy, if we don't act competently.

Our future adults who get results are our only hope to continue directing the greatest nation in the world.   One is remembered for their contributions, such that I want to make a factual difference! I enjoy teaching about conquering difficult challenges.

How can we stay positive in a negative world, this is the question for humanity? I've made a step in the right direction. These scriptures from the Bible demonstrate positivism, i.e., challenged, challenges, differently-abled, multiple intelligence's, over negativism or disability environment terms, i.e., disabled, retarded, handicapped, cripple, etc.

Biblical references for proper terminology: Proverbs 18:21 "Death and life are in the power of the Tongue."; Matthew 12:37 "For by thy words thou shalt be justified, and by thy words thou shalt be Condemned."; Proverbs 23:7 "For as he thinketh in his heart, so is he."; Ps. 12:2 "They speak Vanity every one with his neighbor: with flattering lips and with a double heart do they speak."; John 15:7 "If ye abide in me, and my words abide in you, ye shall ask what ye will, and it shall be done unto You."; Eph 6:17 "the sword of the Spirit, which is the word of God."; First Thess. 5:8 "But let us, who are of the day, be sober, putting on the breastplate of faith and love; and for a helmet, the hope of salvation."; Romans 12:14 "Bless them that persecute you; bless and curse not."; "Death and life are in the power of the tongue." Pro. 18:21 "As he hath called you is holy, so be ye holy in all manner of conversation". 1 Peter 1:15 "Having, therefore these promises dearly beloved, let us cleanse ourselves from all filthiness of the flesh and spirit, perfecting holiness in the fear of God." 2 Cor. 7:1 "By him therefore let us offer the sacrifice of praise to God continually, that is, the fruit of our lips giving thanks to his name." Heb 13:15 "The wicked is snared by the transgression of his lips: but the just shall come out of trouble." Proverbs 12:13.

Looking at these cruel/inhumane terms, which are defined negatively (Year-1983): disable (15c) means "to deprive of legal right, qualification, or capacity; to make incapable or ineffective; to deprive of physical, moral, or intellectual strength. disabled (1633) means "incapacitated by illness, injury, or wounds"; disadvantage (1534) means "loss or damage esp. to reputation, credit, or; finances; an unfavorable, inferior, prejudicial condition". handicap (1660) means "a race or contest in which an artificial advantage is given or disadvantage imposed on a contestant to equalize chances of winning; a disadvantage that makes achievement unusually difficult". handicapped (1915) means "having a physical or mental retard (1788) means "a holding back of slowing down"; "to slow up esp. by preventing or hindering advance or accomplishment; to delay academic progress by failure to promote". retarded (1895) means "slow of limited in intellectual or emotional development or academic progress". disability (1581) means "the condition of being disabled; inability to pursue an occupation because of physical or mental impairment; lack of legal qualification to do something". This creates a legal fear factor, because no beneficial meanings are allowed or promoted.

Being labeled as disabled initially scared me; because of the imposed negative fear factor. These terms only made me regret that I was alive, because of their imposed negativity on my potential was seen as false/make believe. I saw myself as a failure by these terms, in all that I did, because nothing was earned (glass ceiling) by my skills. I was confused by the disability, because many around me, but not all – family/friends – didn't expect me to do much, seriously. They were content to allow me to assimilate with those, who've been brainwashed by the legal disinformation/sabotage (disabled, retarded, handicapped, etc.) of their potential. This angered me that my family would allow me to be sidelined, because "the thinking was, once the brain is damaged, it can't be healed".

Chapter One

On July 28th, '65 to be exact, I was born to a farming family both of chickens & tomatoes. I had a congenital heart defect, but wasn't able to undergo surgery. As a future adult, I lived an ordinary life. When I was in the second grade, my parents divorced, because of my father's drinking, so the last part of my second grade of school was spent at Vast Elementary School. My mother was allowed to visit us every second weekend. In the state of Swift, a court gave custody to a known drunk over my mother. I and my brother went to spend some time with our mother on September 24th, '77, that day our step-father took us fishing with our mother, but the fish weren't biting, so we returned home to the sawmill where we fooled around riding a three-wheeler, now outlawed, which wasn't in the best of shape, but would run so we had fun riding it in the woods, and mud, like future adults will do. I continued to ride and show out for about thirty minutes until BAM!!!

I was hit by an truck. My brothers said in '78, I lost control of the greasy stringed throttle and it became wrapped around the axle of the back wheels; therefore I lost control of the machine and it ran out of the ditch on to the highway where a vehicle was awaiting my arrival. There are two additional accounts. However, I was killed upon impact. My head left a huge dent in the metal bumper/hood & my brain started swelling! This was the first

Cognitive Challenge (CC). I lived and died continuously on the journey the Emergency Medical Technician's (EMT's) never knowing one minute to another whether I would make the journey or not. My father never lost faith of my recovery; because he stayed by my side in the hospital until I woke up or (so he said). I remained in a coma from September 25th, '77, until around December 15th, '77, roughly 3 months. Doctors of mine have stated that it took two weeks to come out of the deep coma. The injuries I received were a broken left jaw bone, (but I was hit by the truck on the right side of my head), and a broken right pelvis that all healed during the coma. The doctors had their doubts if I would ever wake up or regain consciousness. The cost of the accident was huge, but could have been avoided if I had been wearing a helmet. Mothers' responsibility don't you think, since she had custody over the weekend?

Before the accident, I was very active in all kinds of sports, and I also graduated at the top of my class in the sixth grade. Speaking of sports, I was highly skilled in football, swimming & diving. I had hopes to join (try out for) both the US Olympic team & the US Air Force. These dreams ended, but the Best Quest was just beginning. My mother later denied responsibility of my accident which resulted in cognitive challenges costing $3-5 million dollars & my quality of life. Most of those years, I was on the wrong medication by doctors, because none existed for my cognitive challenged condition. However, when the correct drug combination was found it is great.

The anguish I've suffered has been unpleasant. I was always told that it was my fault for running onto the highway, but in 1995 I found out that the truck ran into me, when I was on the side of the road in our driveway.

There were individuals who would go to school and tease my brother about my condition and some claimed that I had died in the coma. At the innocence age of twelve, I was incorrectly labeled: disabled, a criminal act; forced hatred! Then the doctors said bring his girlfriend up to see him, because at this time it couldn't do any harm. My father presented her to me even though I was looking like death. The biggest smile came over my face that was around December 15th, '77; revitalized. I was allowed to return home for the Christmas holidays. That night after Christmas supper and after the presents were all opened I did what I had prayed I could, I walked from the living room into the kitchen with the whole family watching, to catch if I stumbled or fell. I didn't fall or stumble, imagine that, after that feat I returned to my wheelchair. As my father recalled to me and my family "To just think the doctors said while he was under the coma for such a lengthy period his chances of walking, talking, seeing, feeling, hearing, and breathing, etc., were one in a million". "He is showing signs of a full recovery - he raised his hands to God and tears filled his eyes and everyone there thanked God Almighty." I was proud of my recovered status, not ashamed, so I told everyone of the miracle God had secured through me.

However, this caused many problems, because society doesn't like trauma survivors, I've learned. If I had kept my mouth shut like my father told me in the 1980's, perhaps I would have succeeded earlier? During that time of rehabilitation, where I had to relearn everything down to the most basic function, this took about 2 months of intensive rehabilitation. Unfortunately, I was sent home to my family, who hated me & wished I had not recovered these were daily statements for about 6 years, however, if my mother had obtained custody of me, I would have been sent to an institution, where I would have been forced to be non-productive & this story would have never been! God is right, always!!

Truly, my father and brother persecuted me in ways no one should ever be subjected to especially after a cognitive challenge: hitting me in the head with tomatoes, sticks, hands, and boards to punish me, because of my poor memory & slowness, denied adequate treatment or medication, etc. The years from 1978-1983, every summer we harvested tomatoes for the market, which was about one month. Those summers were spent picking tomatoes. I drove the tractor & my father & brother would pick the tomatoes, but when I would mess up driving, they would throw tomatoes at my head for punishment. My father blamed all of his problems on me for having the accident. It wasn't my fault! However, he convinced me that it was. This lead to vengeance on my part, or bitterness, which wasn't solved until the correct medications Lamictal & Invega in 2007.

As I returned home for good on March 10, '78, upon re-entering school at Joy-Taylor I had to deal with learning challenges, peer pressure, prejudice, betrayal of friends and family, peer ridicule, and discrimination throughout my formative years. My father wouldn't allow institutionalization to happen or the judge who gave him custody. I was thankful that the principal allowed me to advance to the seventh grade, no questions asked, so I could be with my own peer group. I was on no medication, '79-'88, besides for a short period in '86 of Valium; Dilantin.

Which was prescribed by my doctors in Little Rock from age 14 to 23, not one day passed that I did not contemplate suicide or worse. Suicide was reinforced by my being paranoid or always looking over my shoulder for blame, because I was always doing something wrong, forgetting, etc. It is amazing that I functioned without proper medications. I didn't think that I was disabled; therefore I had a positive mindset that I could achieve anything, referring to Almighty Gods' Word, "All things are possible". As school progressed, my grades were high enough to keep me on the honor roll, not all the time but mostly, and every now and then I would get on the superior honor roll. I
received no special education during school, skipped the 7th grade, and graduated with a 3.26 GPA (Grade Point Average), from 1978-1983 with positive absence episodes happening all the time! It's possible to succeed with cognitive challenges. It needs to be shown for the record that I got up at 3 & 4 am to study for some of my exams in high school. This saved you about $90,000, compared to

institutionalization for 6 years. Also during my last year of
school, I was more accepted and suicide was not a constant threat
but only ever now & then, just 3 or 4 times a day. I soon started
experimenting with legal & illegal drugs like Alcohol, Marijuana,
Uppers/Downers, which led to Cocaine, LSD, etc., in college, but I
eventually quit all of these drugs in 1988, cold turkey!!

After I graduated high school in the spring of '83, I went to
college at a university where I again encountered ignorant
individuals who loved to persecute me with name calling and
laughter, but I persevered on. Attaining this degree was not easy
because I had to work, support myself, at both
industries, food management, and the Center. During my last year of
school at the first university I was taking fifteen hours of
classes, I also worked forty-seventy two hours at a defense
plant/factory, & I was involved in a Hollywood Play, with no proper
medication for any of my cognitive challenges.

While I was working at the industry in '86, three men broke into my
home & tried to kill me. Gods' grace was with me again. They
dragged me off the bed onto the floor by my heels & beat me in the
head. I was taking Valium, doctor prescribed; because of my nerves
the night the trio came to visit. My brother asked me to get him a
job at industry, since I had such a great work record. I did, he
eventually went to college at my second university, when he needed a
job, I came through or delivered for him. My own brother who
watched me break my back to work & be accepted, said "I was brain
damaged & couldn't do the work.", when I asked him to assist me get
work in 1997.

When I returned from the streets (homelessness) in '87 my step-
father, who fixed up the three-wheeler allowed me to stay at his
house for a very limited time. This resulted, because my parent
(mother) did not want me to achieve anything, but rather relinquish
my mental & physical state to their control like
many others around the world, where they could collect money for my
dependency & suppression.

However, I soon was forced to move out because her husband. I soon
found a job, thus not homeless. This truth that I've realized is
obtainable by all cause God has a purpose for all of us, I believe:
"All is possible, if you dare to be the Best". There are some who
never try, because I've meet them & told them that they could do it,
but they will not fight their family, which is necessary. Also,
living like I have had to do, since viewed as disabled and
incompetent, since the wreck, even after receiving two college
degrees, an associate & bachelor, makes you wonder why
rehabilitation spent all of that money to save my life?   Sometimes
these episodes can control your life, but I was able to conquer this
incident that was placed upon me. I feel others can too, if they
know that success can be achieved.

It would be '88 before I would get any kind of medication for my
challenges, because I was mis-diagnosed with these wrong diseases,

i.e., '88-'92, Epilepsy, Alzheimer, Organic Brain Disorder (a terminal illness & given 6 months to live), Schizophrenia, Seizure Disorder, etc., all of which were disabling/incorrect. When this happened, I quit the drug scene immediately, because you don't mix drugs. I have been placed on numerous medications by several physicians whose aim it was to keep me, dependent upon them for drugs. Do you know how detrimental getting a death sentence can be to your life, especially when it's wrong? When I got this statement, I realized that I didn't have long to live. Therefore, I started a popular habit, called dipping snuff. I did quit when I learned that these drugs do not mix well with my medications, either! I was scared from all that had happened, but I continued on my positive mission for God, helmets can save lives, if used!! Many friends abandon you, because you lie or mislead. These wrong diagnoses continued until recently, the challenge I suffer is absence episodes (momentary stares) which are of a positive & benign type or positive seizures.

Dr. Que, my doctor, in '89 stated that I was disabled, due to my brain injury! He assisted me in getting a job at the store, because he was on the Board of Directors. My suicide thoughts were a constant memory, which I've had to battle every day, until 2007. I took Dilantin, (according to doctor records) for about one year after I was released in March, '78, then Dr. Que terminated the drug in '79. I was consequently, forced to quit/fired from the store in August of '89. This would have not happened, if my doctor had taken proper care of me, which was his job! After the store fired me, my first thought was "What do I do, since I cannot work", along with this negative perspective or defamation of character? Being fired isn't fun, especially when you are not on the correct medication. It can destroy your confidence & desire to succeed. Mrs. Paula told me that I should go to college, but I said if I can't remember, what is the purpose? She said "You'll never know until you try". I told her I already had one college degree, but it was of no value. She said "They had to fire me, because I couldn't do the job". The store reinforced my disability by assisting me to get on disability. I was not disabled to begin with, but that is what can happen to individuals who have little or no education. That is why I attempt with all my existence to change this negative perspective to a positive, because somewhere in the future, one human individual who has not been limited or denied access will direct our nation to be the champion of all those who've ever existed. The store reinforced my being helpless by brainwashing me to believe, that I was disabled & that I could never work because, no one would hire me. It being a small town, it wasn't long before everyone in the town and now 30 years later, everyone who knows me feels that I am brain disabled. This can disable your chances of getting a job, regardless of the amount of college you have. Mrs. Paula made some calls to the Rehabilitative Services. Mr. Jones was my contact. I got together with him a few days later & due to my accident in '77, I was eligible to go to college free starting in August, '89, & they said they'll help me find work, when I graduated. This has been untrue since '93! First, I thank the taxpayers all very much. Mr. Baxter told me & my wife "that no one will hire you because of your seizures". There has been no change, since I've told them I no longer/never had seizures. Many people need to know that seizures can be positive & beneficial, like mine.

During the early '90's I became involved with the Trauma Association. Since then the name has changed to the Head Association, they say this title is better for us or more positive, I was on the Board of Directors for some years. During that time I made a lot of suggestions about awareness & media coverage of successes/positive role models like Dr. Advar, President, Head Association, & I to show others that success after Congitive Challenges is possible. You never know who or how your positive position will aspire others. Life is great, because most people think being brain damaged is always negative, but it's not! This is definitely not the case for me! More should accomplish success like I've done, because it is possible, regardless of your cognitive challenges!

I need to share with you the difficulties that I've encountered in obtaining employment, because I am referred to as disabled by these organizations, which were set up to promote the capabilities of the disabled. They, our government, saw fit to do this, but I ask you what they were trying to achieve?

Chapter Two

People who were thought of as my friends started calling me self-limiting or negative names/titles/labels like; i.e., (disability environment terms) disabled, cripple, handicap, limply, half-a-man, disadvantaged, odd ball, geek, and retarded, which our federal government has legally authorized! It was not long after my return home that my thoughts turned to suicide, because television promotes incompetency for those with Cognitive Challenges. This unlawful abuse happens every day to so many, roughly another 20 million individuals by 2010 ($40 trillion dollars). What will you do, when it happens to you? Remember you have less than 60 minutes to act or your chances of a full recovery are slim. My wife is amazed at the abuse I survived allowed by both the state & my family!

Then in '92 I was correctly guided by the hand of God to find Dr. May address at Dr. Fred's office and I went to see her in Memphis. She sent me to Dr. Field. I took the time & effort to try and patch relations between me & my father by taking him with me to see Dr. Field & learn about my challenge. He condemned me all the way back, a trip of about 150 miles. Such that I almost kicked him out of my truck & forced him to walk home. However, I'm not that cruel.

In '92, I started looking for work, since I was to graduate in '93 through a magazine called "Careers & The Disabled" which guaranteed me a job, because there employers hired the disabled, disadvantaged, handicapped, etc., or so they said. I filled out the enclosed

letter that the magazine included for the disabled or handicapped
person to include to the prospective employer.
I contacted all Fortune 500 companies in '92 & '93, in '92 I was
contacted by 113 (22.6%) employers; Companies and Names of Contacts
Years 1992 and 1993 Magazine: "Careers & the disABLED" (113
Responses Out of 500 Careers Applications Sent)

Playtex Family Products Corporation, CT, Marybeth Fiorelli
Shearson Lehman Brothers, DC, Peter Scudner
ICI Americas Inc., DE, NN
Delco Electronics, GM Hughes Electronics, IN, NN
The Doctors' Company, CA, Joan Bowyer
EDS, TX, Jane Allston
Eli Lilly and Company, Ron L. Anglea
Merck, NJ, Cheryl Pavich Sabath, AAron L. Walker
Smithkline Beecham, PA, Lauralyn Jones
AETNA, CT, Maureen Ryan
Xerox, AR, Nord Foster
ITT Hartford, CT, Gregory A. Ashford
Novell, UT, Patricia G. Ellison
McDonnell Douglas Technical Services Company, CA, NN
Bechtel, MD, Liska L. Brown
Burlington Industries, Inc., NC, Tony Michaels
Liberty Mutual, MA, Dennis W. Nicholls
UPS, GA, NN
GenCorp Aerojet, MS, Kathy Lucas
Winrock International, AR, Deborah Smith
National Health Insurance Company, TX, Guy Davie
Texas Instruments, TX, Dave Current
Wal Mart, AR, Randy Hickman
UGI Corporation, PA, Kathleen A. Cashin
Promus Companies, TN, Lisa Edenton
La Quinta Motor Inns, TX, Anne Binns
Belk Stores Services, NC, Tom Westall
Molex Incorporated, AR, Greggory Dyess
Milliken, SC, Paul Loadholdt
Motel 6, TX, Erin Arroyo
Abbott Laboratories, IL, Jean Jackson-Swopes
Bristol-Myers Squibb Company, IN, Yvette R. Payne
Baxter Healthcare Corporation, IL, NN
Rockwell International, CA, NN
Martin Marietta Energy Systems, TN, NN
Kaiser Permanente, CA, Thomas Peebles
AmTran Corporation, AR, John Mattox
Hallmark Cards, MO, Tim Moran
Microsoft, WA, NN
Hewlett Packard, CA, NN
Honeywell, Inc., FL, Pamela Bowman
Nathan's Famous, Inc., NY, Karen Brown
Sterling Winthrop, NY, Cassandra Philippeaux
Bristol-Squibb Company, NY, NN
Rockwell International, CA, NN
Baxter Healthcare Corp., IL, NN
Coca Cola Foods, TX, Ghary Gibbs

Martin Marietta, FL, Bruce Czarniak
Pfizer, NY, Faye Williams
General Data Comm, Inc., CT, David Alley
Exxon, TX, NN
Cargill, MN, Campbell
Boots Pharmaceuticals, LA, NN
Liberty Mutual Insurance, MA, Dineena ONeal
National Saftey Associates, TN, Michael Farraris
Arkansas Epilepsy Society, AR, Nancy Weinberger
Colgate-Palmolive Co., NY, John Garrison
Met Life, NY, NN
MA General Hospital, MA, NN (2)
Veda, VA, NN
Payless Cashways, MO, NN
Sears, Roebuck and Co., IL, RT Harwood
Glaxo Inc., NC, Sue Spicer
Household Credit Services, Inc., CA, NN
Hewlett Packard, CA, NN
Motel 6, NN
Department of Pollution Control and Ecology, AR, Donna Cox (2)
Kroger, OH, Terry Kuhl
Monsanto, MO, RJ Mason
Cigna, PA, NN
Salomon Brothers, Inc., NY, Jackie Fasitta
Colgate-Palmolive Company, NY, John Garrison
Marshall Field's, IL, David Kowalczyk
Aluminum Company of America, PA, NN
Hallmark Cards, MO, Tim Moran
Cellular One, AR, NN
KATV Television, AR, Sharon Lewis
AAFES, TX, Karen Smith
First Interstate, CA, Katie Vinnicombe
Kellogg's, MI, Bill Steele
Worthen Bank, AR, Brenda Hester
Campbell Soup, NJ, Patricia Spruill
Jerrico, KY, Carol Caskey
Upjohn, MI, MW Johnson
SRI Specialty Retailers, Inc., TX, Carolann Moore
The Timken Company, OH, Lloyd M. Groves
Booz Allen & Hamilton, Inc., CA, Kelley Brown
Amoco Corporation, IL, Daniel Harper
Burdines, Donna Magee
Pillsbury, MN, Scott Patterson
Johnson & Johnson, NJ, Judith Talbott
HE Butt Grocery Company, TX, Linda Gabbard
Phillips Petroleum Company, OK, EL Baughn
Champion, CT, John L. Lewis
Del Monte Foods, CA, Betty A. Lyle
Kimberly-Clark Corporation, AR, Gary W. Short
Ralston Purina Company, MO, Tim J. Toma
Wrangler, NC, Jeannette Davies
Costal HealthCare Group, Inc., NC, NN
National Steel, IN, Ken Scullion
Computer Associates, NN

Citizens Bank, AR, D. Keith Hefner
AEL Industries, Inc., PA, Matt Ludlow
Bechtel Corporation, MD, Katherine E. Hand
Fannie Mae, DC, NN
White Lodging Services Corporation, IN, John Januszko
BASF Corporation, NJ, Jerome C. Wichinsky
Arkansas, The Natural State, AR, David Williams
Computer Sciences Corporation, VA, Jacqueline Lemon
Ball Corporation, IN, Rhonda L. Thomas
National Semiconductor, CA, NN
Captain D's, TN, George Neal

1993 (61 Responses Out of 500 Careers Applications Sent)

Lincoln Electric, OH, Paul Beddia
Army & Air Force Exchange Service, TX, Karen Smith
Toyota Motor Manufacturing, KY, No Name
AR State Spinal Cord Commission, AR, Cheryl Vines, Patti Rogers
Univ. of AR, Fayetteville, Cathy Renner, Kay Trumbo
UCA, AR, Logan Hampton, Dana Lynch
AR College, Clarinda Foote
ASU, Tom Trevathan,
Univ. of AR, Tom Dorre
AR Small Business Development Center, AR, Victor Redditt
Human Services, AR, Lavell Wilbanks
Ouachita Technical Institute, AR, Susan Prugh
Jay Dickey, AR, House of Reps.
Univ. of the Ozarks, AR, Judy Alexander, Gene Stephenson,
The Woods Service, PA
AR Easter Seals, AR, Melvin Johnston
Westark Community College, AR, Beverly Gilstrap
Department of the Navy, MD
Phillip Morris, NY, Raymond Fusco
Beverly Enterprises, AR, Pat Powell
ICAN, AR, Sue Guskin
Mainstream Living, AR, Judy Edwards
UALR, AR, Susan Queller
UAMS, AR, H. Jones
South AR Community College, AR, Nancy Werst
Hewlett Packard, CA, No Name
Apple Computer, Inc., CA, No Name
Independent Case Mgmt., AR, Becky Johnson
Intel, CA, No Name
Marriott, DC, No Name
Nestle Food Company, CA, No Name
ITT, MN, No Name
Eastman Kodak Company, NY, NN "No Name"
Best Western International, AZ, NN
Arkansas The Natural State, AR, David Williams
Pitney Bowes, CT, Linda Higueras
Merck, Inc., Anthony D. Rizzello
General Electric, CT, Elaine M. Phillips
Warren Lambert, NJ, Maria Gagnier

Prudential, NJ, Sharon Taylor
Baxter Healthcare Corporation, IL, Terry Recht (I called)
JCPenney, TX, Roy Chapman
Coca Cola Foods, TX, Ghary Gibbs
Parke-Davis, TX, ME Moran, LB Slater
Microsoft, WA, Debbie Stanley
Eli Lilly and Company, IN, Ron Anglea
Novell, UT, NN
Honeywell, MN, Ann Sherman
RehabCare Corporation, MO, Sean Melonz
Pitney Bowes, CT, Guss Stepp, Jr.
Red Lobster, FL, Larry Gray
Hyatt Hotels and Resorts, IL, Chuck Palid
American Honda Motor Co., Inc., CA, Sharon Thompson
Procter and Gamble, OH, B. Arnold
Xerox Corporation, Theodore E. Payne
Arthur Andersen, IL, Dennis R. Reigle
American Management Systems, VA, Eric Schlesinger
Smithkline Beecham, PA, Patricia Friel
Texas Instruments, Dave Current
Mead, OH, Donna P. Chapman
Warren Lambert, NJ, NN; none with a job offer, then in '93 I re-
contacted the Fortune 500 companies and I was contacted by only 61
(12.2%) employers, none with a job offer. I contacted 97 more
companies in '96 with the same outcome of no employment. I also
have contacted many hundreds of employers (exceeding 560) with
certified mail about employment opportunities & possible sponsorship
with no beneficial outcome. Responses were low like those reflected
above.

CERTIFIED Letters Sent Out Looking for Sponsorship/Work; Neither
occurred.

(546 or costing over $1709) NZ= no zip code & no address.110 plus
names

The First Church of Christ, 175 Huntington Ave., Boston, MA, 02115
Oct 26, 94
Mr. Gayle Morris, Oct. 26, '94
Vantage Press, 516 W. 34th St., NY 10001 Oct. 26, '94
Keith Alexander, Cloiborne Parish School Board, PO Box 600, Homer,
LA 71040 Oct. 26, '94
Edward Kennedy, 315 Russell Bldg. DC 20510 9/20/94
Carole Hettema, PO Box 980048, Richmond, VA 23298-0048 10/13/94
Dun & Bradstreet, 3 Sylvan WAY, Parsippany, NJ 11/1/94
Radio-TV News Director Ass, 1717 St. NW, Ste. 615, DC 11/1/94
Bob Wingfield, 11/1/94
1) Glen Amason, 11/1/94

Dr.Eva Bartolos, Diplomates, 1534 Elizabeth Ste. 111, Shreveport,
LA 71101 11/1/94
Main Street Magnolia, Ms. Neca Reap, Box 1153, Magnolia, AR 71753
11/1/94

Medical Care International, 5080 Spectrum, Dallas, TX 75248-6433
11/1/94
Medical Group Management, 1355 S. Colorado Suite 900, Denver, CO
80222-3300 11/1/94
Medical World News Magazine, 500 Howard St., SF, CA 94105-3000
11/1/94
UCA, UCA PO Box 4937, Conway, AR 72035 11/1/94
Mayo Clinic, 200 SW First St., Rochester, MN 55905-0001 11/1/94
Princeton University, One Washington Rd., Princeton, NJ 08544
11/1/94
Media Span, PO Box 40930, Indianapolis, IN 46245-0930 11/1/94
2) Medical Econ. Magazine, 680 Kenderkamads Rd., Oradell, NJ 07649-
     1696 11/1/94

Medical Ass. Inc., 1 Cycor Pl., Ste. 230, Dubuque, IA 52001-0000
11/1/94
Electonic Now, 5008 BiCo Blvd., Farmingdale, NY 11735 11/1/94
Sanford, Beshear, PO Box 487, Rison, AR 71665 11/1/94
Dun & Bradstreet, 299 Park Ave., NY 10171-0096 11/1/94
Prof. Charles Fort, 5 Connecticut State University, New Haven, CT
06515 11/23/94
R. Gwergin, Tufts University, Medford, MA 02155 11/23/94
G. Keeley, Harvard, Cambridge, MA 02138 11/23/94
Dr. Marilyn McGrath, Harvard, Cambridge, MA 02138 11/22/94
Nancy Collins, MIT Personnel, MA 02139-4307 11/22/94
3) Tiffany Franklin, 1202 W. Walnut St., Prescot, AR 71857 11/22/94

93 KISQ Radio Station, 2525 NW Ave., El Dorado, AR 71730 11/22/94
Capital Cities, (ABC) 77W 66th St., NY 10023-6295 12/16/94
Ozark Publishing, PO Box 489, Mineral Spring, TX 76068 12/16/94
Walt Disney Company, 500 S. Buena Vista St., Burbank, CA 91521-
000112/16/94
Christa McAuliffe, 1201 16th St. NW, DC 20036 12/12/94
Graduating Engineer, 16030 Ventura Blvd., Encino, CA 91436 12/12/94
Milton Petrie, Petrie Stores, 70 Enterprise Ave., Secaucus, NJ 07094
12/12/94
Miami Dolphins, 2269 NW 199th St., Miami, FL 33056 12/12/94
George Gleason, Ozark Bank, Main Branch, Ozark, AR 72949 12/12/94
4) James Brady, NHIF, 333 Turnpike Rd., Southboro, MA 01772
     12/12/94

America's Talking, 2200 Fletcher Ave., Ft. Lee, NJ 07024 1/12/95
Dewayne Graham, 7 on your Side, PO Box 77, Little Rock, AR 72203
1/12/95
Charles Scribner's Sons, Mr. Ned Chese, 866 Third Ave., NY 10022
1/16/95
American Teacher Awards, PO Box 9805, Calabasas, CA 91372 1/16/95
Home Depot, Director, 2727 Paces Ferry Rd. NW, Atlanta, GA 30339
1/16/95
Office Depot, Inc., 851 Broken Sound Pkwy NW, Bacon Raton, FL 33487
1/16/95
Dorothy Skeel, 3501 Newardk St., DC 20016 1/19/95
Cambridge University Press, The Elinburgh Bldg., Cambridge, England,
Mr. J. England, Reg. # 611593390, Oct 25/94

Education Week, 4301 Connecticut Ave., DC, 20008 11/3, '94
5) Ms. Deborah Warner, The Washington Center, Deborah Warner, DC,
    20005, Nov. 3, '94

Shutesbury Elem. School, 23 West Pehlm, Shutesbury, MA, 01072
1/24/95
Technology & Learning, 2169 Franciso Blvd., E 86-A4, San Ratfael,
CA, 94901 1/24/95
The Wall Street Journal, 200 Liberty St., NY, 10281 1/24/95
Dixie Lawrence, LA, 1724 N Burnside #7, Gonzales, LA 70737 1/24/95
Tufts University, Dean Grad., Medford, MA 02155 MA, 1/24/95
Chronicle, DC, 1255 23rd St., NW, DC 20037 1/24/95
Fellowship International Committee, Rt. 1 Box 155, Rutledge, MO,
63563 1/24/95
Richard Baldwin, MI, 2500 Kerr St. Ste. 208, Lansing, MI 48912
1/24/95
Judy Baker, 295 Longwood Center, Boston, MA 02115 1/24/95
6) Vicki Carr Scholarship, PO Box 5126, Beverly Hills, CA 90210
    2/8/95

Boys & Girls Club of America, 1230 W. Peachtree St., NW, Atlanta, GA
30309 2/6/95
Phil Hardin Fdn, PO Box 187, Meridian, MS 39302 2/6/95
Arnenborg Fdn, PA 150 Rodner©Chester Rd., St. Davids, PA 19807
2/6/95
Consortium of College of University Media, 121 Pearson Hall, Ames,
IA 50011-2203 2/6/95
The Polaroid Fdn, 750 main St. 2N, Canlindy, MA 02139 2/6/95
JP Getty Fdn, 401 Wilshire Blvd., Ste. 1000, San Monica, CA 90401-
1455 2/6/95
Fred & Mary Koch Fdn, PO Box 2256, Wichita, KS 67201 2/6/95
The Quorem for American Future, 174 Idlewilds Dr., Winstom-Salem, NC
27106 2/6/95
Hershey Foods Corp. Fund, 100 Crystal A Dr., Hershey, PA 17033
7) W. Alton Jones, Fdn., 323 E High St., Charolettesville, VA
    22902-5178

Deloitte & Touche Fdn., Ten We Sport Rd., Wilton, CT 06897
Weyerhauser Fdn., Clt 1 F31, Tacoma, WA 98477
Texas Instruments, Ms. Ann Minsus, Grant Adm., PO Box 650311-M/S
53906, Dallas, TX 75265
Educational Fdn of America, 23161 Ventura Blvd., Woodland Hills, CA
91364
School Mayo Study Group, 860 18th Ave., Salt Lake City, UT 84103
FSC Fdn, 555 N. Lombard Rd., Addison, IL 60101, 2/3/95
Radio & TV News Fdn, 1000 Conn. Ave NW, Washington, DC 20036
GTE Fdn, 1 Stamford Forum, Stamford, CT 06904
Sara Lee Fdn, 31st Nat. Plaza Chicago, IL 60602
8) Ross Fdn, PO Box 335, Arkadelphia, AR 71923

Nichols Fdn, PO Box 5667, NLR, AR 72219
Kenan Trust, PO Box 3858, Chapel Hill, NC
Beth Anne Rankin, Miss Arkansas, 5807 Shallow Cove, NLR, AR 72118
Hussman Fdn, PO Box 2221, LR, AR 72203

Regenstein Fdn, 8600 W Bryn Macor Ave., Chicago, IL 60631
Norris Fdn, 11 Golden Shore Ste 450, Long Beach, CA 90802
Koch Fdn, 2830 NW 41st St Ste 4, Gainesville, FL 32606
National Medical Enterprise Fdn, 11620 Wilshire Blvd., PO Box 25980, LA, CA 90025
Reader's Digest Fdn, CL Edwards, Pleasantville, NY 10570
90) Josiah Macy Fdn, 44E 64th St., NY 10021

Warren Lambert Co. Fdn, 201 Talbot Rd., Morris Plain, NJ 07950
Kazanjiian Economics Fdn., 16 Cleft Rock Lane, Woodbridge, CT 06515
New York Fd., Empire State Bldg #2901, NY 10036
Koch Fdn, 1401 I St. Ste 300, DC 20005
Tyson, Donald Wray, PO Box 2020, Springdale, AR 72765-2020
Bristol-Myers Fdn., 345 Park Ave., NY 10154
Anheuser Bush Fdn, One Busch Pl. St. Louis, MO 63118
Department of Education, 400 Maryland Ave. SW, DC 20202
Southern Educational Fdn., 135 Auburn Ave., NE, Atlanta, GA 30303
100) Graco Fdn, PO Box 1441, Minneapolis, MN 55440-1441

Rockefellar Fdn, Ms. Lynda Mullen, Sec., 420 5th Ave., NY 10018-2702
Capital Cities/ABC Fdn., Mr. Thomas S. Murphy, 24 E. 51st St., NY 10022
House of St. Giles the Cripple, One Hanson Pl., Brooklyn, NY 11217
Henry Ball Foundation, 9600 San Monica Blvd., Beverly Hills, CA 90210
Rockefellar Brother's Fdn, Mr. Benjamin Shute, Jr. Sec., 1290 Ave. of the America's, NY 10104
Paul & Mary Haus Fdn, 600 Leopard St., Ste 1400, Corpus Christi, TX 78401
Blackwell Fdn. Trust, 1400 W. 43rd St., Pine Bluff, AR 71603
Commonwealth Fund, One E. 75th St., NY 10021-2692
Grace Fdn, One Toun Center Rd., Bacon Raton, FL 33486-1010
110) Stanley Fdn, 1402 Hendricks Blvd., Fort Smith, AR 72901

Archer Daniels Midland Fdn, 4666 Faries Pkwy., Decatur, IL 62525
Frank Hickingbotham, 425 W. Capitol Ste. 1100, LR, AR 72201
Roy G. Mitchell Fdn, 1100 N. Woodard St., Birmingham, MI 48011
Sawyer Charitable Fdn, 209 Columbus Ave. 5th Fl., Boston, MA 02116
KMart Fdn, Corporate Contributions, 310 W. Big Beaver Rd., Troy, MI 48084-3163
Kimberly Clark Fdn, PO box 619100, Dallas, TX 75261-9100
Danforth Fdn, 231 South Bemiston, St. Louis, MO 63105
Charles Stewart Mott Fdn, 1200 Mott Found. Bildg., Flint, MI 48502-1851
Joan Kroc Fdn, Ms. Elizabeth Benes, 8939 Villa La Jolla Dr., Ste. 201, La Jolla, CA 92037
120) JE & LE Mabee Fdn, Ms. Gay Mabee, Chairman, 3000 Mid Contient Tower, Tulsa, OK 74103

AH Kerr Fdn, Mr. Robert S. Kerr, Jr., 6301 NWestern Ste. 130, Oklahom City, OK 73118
E. Faith Wade Endowment, 114 E. DelaGuena St., Santa Barbara, CA 93101

Dow Jones Fdn, Mr. Leonard Doherty, Admin., 200 Liberty St., NY 10281
Hasbro Children's Fdn, 32 West 23rd St., NY 10010
Robert & Helen Kleberg Fdn, Mr. Robert Washington, Adm., 700 N. St. Mary's St., Ste. 1200, San Antonio, TX 76904
Lilly Endowment, Program Officer, 2801 N. Meridian St., PO Box 88068, Indianapolis, IN 46208
Procter & Gamble Fdn, PO Box 599, Cincinnati, OH 45201-0599
Open Society Fund, Inc., 10 Columbia Circle Rm. 1230, NY 10019
Keebler Fdn, One Hallow Tree Lane, Elmhurst, IL 60126
130) Walton Fdn, 125 W. Central Suite 210, Bentonville, AR 72712

Hewlett Packard Co. Fdn, 3000 Hanover St., Palo Alto, CA 94304
Educational Ford Foundation, 199 Wickenden St., Providence, RI 02903
Hewlett Foundation, 525 Middlefield Ste. 200, Mennle Park, CA 94025Broward Educational Fdn, Ms. Katherine B. Doberman, Trea., 1320 Southwest 4th St., Fort Lauderdale, FL 33312
Joseph P Kennedy Jr. Fdn, 1350 NY Ave, NW, DC 20005-4709
Rosalie Tilles Child Home Fdn, 315 N. 7th St., Fort Smith, AR 72901
Roy & Christine Sturgis Fdn, NCNB Texas Box 83500, Dallas, TX 75283
Murphy Fdn, Murphy Building, El Dorado, AR 71730
Boston Globe Fdn, PO Box 2378, Boston, MA 02107
140) Olin Fdn, 780 3rd Ave., Suite 3403, NY 10017-7090 2/6/95

American Council Rural Special Education, 221 Milton Bennison Hall, Salt Lake City, UT 84112 2/8/95
Bellsouth Foundation, 1155 Peachtree St., Atlanta, GA 30367 2/8/95
National Ass. Craniofacially Handicapped, PO Box 11082, Chattonooga, TN 37401 2/8/95
Beth Ann Rankin, Miss Arkansas, 5807 Shadow Cove, NLR, AR 72118 2/8/95
Mrs. Haynes, Gill High, Texarkana, AR 75502 2/8/95
Kilgore, TX, Mr. Dana M. Ransom, 1100 Broadway, (Rangerettes) 75662 2/6/95
St Michaels, Texarkana, TX 75502 2/13/95
Kenneth Stewart, Rt. Box 127-A, Ozan, AR 71855 2/13/95
Wal Mart Corp, PO Box 116, Bentonville, AR 72712-9956 2/13/95
150) Jerry Martin, 742 Van Gogh St., Fayettville, AR 72703 2/13/95

Oprah, PO Box 909715, Chicago, IL 60690 2/13/95
Homer Best, 23 Alexander Ave. #104, Merced, CA 2/13/95
Jay Gibson, 1200-B Oak Hill, White Hall, AR 71602 2/13/95
Keith Alexander, PO Box 600, Homer, LA 71040 2/13/95
Richard F. Elmos, 409 Guitman Library, Cambridge, MA 02138 2/13/95
Matthew Ruston, 6708 Hill Park Drive #403, LA, CA 90068 2/13/95
Main St. Magnolia, Mrs. Necca Reco, Box 1153, McAlgter Buld. Ste. 305, Magnolia, AR 71753 2/13/95
Dr. Bartolas, 1534 Elizabeth, Suite 111, Shreveport, LA 71101 2/13/95
National School Board, 1680 Dunn Street, Alexandria, VA 22314 2/13/95
160) Dr. Marshall Smith, Dean, Stanford University, Stanford, CA 94305 2/13/95

National Association of Secondary Principals, President, 1904 Ass.
Drive, Reston, VA 22091 2/13/95
Association for Supervision & Curriculum Development, Executive
Director, 1250 N. Pitt St., Alexandria, VA 22314 2/13/95
Cassey's Countdown, Mr. David Perry, Hollowood, CA 90078 2/13/95
Reader's Digest, Pleasantville, NY 10570 2/13/95
Prackker Publications, Inc, Managing Editor, 275 Melty Dr., Ste. 1,
PO Box 8623, Ann Arbor, MI 48107 2/13/95
John F. Kennedy School of Gov. at Harvard, Susan Lusi, Malcolm
Wiener Center for Social Policy, 79 JFK Street, Cambridge, MA 02138
2/13/95
Stanford University, Diane Massell, , School of Education, Stanford,
CA 94305 2/13/95
Teaching K-8, Mr. Allen Raymond, 2300 W. 5th Ave., Columbus, OH
43216 2/13/95
Independent Institute, Director, 134 98th Ave., Dept. GF2, Oakland,
CA 94603 2/13/95
170) Springhouse Corporation, Ms. Maryanne Wagner, 1111 Bethlem
Pike, PO Box 908, Sprinhouse, PA 19477 2/13/95

Ema Fdn. Awards, Director, C/O School Match, 5027 Pink Creek Dr.,
Westerville, OH 43081 OH 2/13/95
National Association of Boards of Education, 1012 Cameron St.,
Alexandria, VA 22314 2/13/95
MSU, Dr. James Spillane, College ofEducation, MSU, Erickson Hall,
East Landing, MI 48824 2/13/95
Gail Hinkel, Managing Editor, 1507 E. Broadway, Columbia, MO 65211
2/13/95
Stanford Beshear, , PO Box 487, Rison, AR 71665 2/13/95
Ass. Dir. of Student Affairs, PO Box 4937, Conway, AR, 72032 2/13/95
Beverly Brunt, Rt. 1 Box 442, Perlisville, VT, 05151 2/13/95
Mac Short, 110 Elden St., Heindar, VA 22070 2/13/95
Arkansas Magazine 800 Hotz Hall, Fayetteville, AR 72701 2/17/95
180) Teachers Cert. Station, State of OK, Ok City OK 73105 2/17/95

In '93 my suicidal thoughts diminished. Perhaps, because I was
finally being treated human by most people! After the diagnosis in
'92 by Dr. Field, my grade point average (GPA) went from 2.6 to 3.3
the first semester of my last year and 3.7 the following semester,
this was my final year as an undergraduate. On May 15, '93, I
graduated from the second university, with a Bachelor of Science in
Business Management with a 2.61 GPA. During my college days at the
second university, I was again like in high school, falsely accused
of raping a female, etc. Needless to say my last three years of
college were an experience; phone calls which hung up on me, death
threats, daily confrontation with the enemies, and mysterious
relationships (trusting few because others loved to stab you in the
back) or harassment. The last year was quiet different. Why? The
medication change was the key, because many students saw a positive
change & even my professors. Another reason I got irritated with
many individuals feeling they were better than I, because I was
classified as disabled, which is negative, I saw the need for a
positive perspective thus I started an organization "Challenged

Conquistadors, Inc" (CC). I founded, "CC", a nonprofit incorporated support group for challenged students & the public. Paul states in "The Bible", Romans 8:37 "Nay, in all these things we are more than conquerors through him that loved us." This is where "Challenged Conquistadors, Inc." were born. The goals of the group have many purposes: First, do away with negative terminology, which is used to legally discriminate, etc., and 2) to educate the public of the many positive and productive contributions, 3) the cognitively challenged can contribute to our society, 4) given the opportunity; 5) to educate the challenged to the many opportunities that exist to regain independence, 6) to assist with the integration into society's work force, 7) stress the value of helmets, and 8) to empower the challenged to become self-supportive, taxpaying, and invaluable citizens that they are capable of becoming. I want to tell you, people who laughed at me, called me names, threatened me, and hated me started respecting, listening, and appreciating the efforts I had started to raise awareness that yes I am different, but I can be your greatest asset or your worst liability, your decision! Which you have to live with: either employ us at your industries, or support us through social dependency programs. However, I have not obtained any of their support since graduation; apparently their opinions were only lip service.

I started looking for someone/company to fund my new idea. I spent a huge amount of time at libraries all over the state, e.g., trying to secure the best information to present to foundations regarding my opportunity of positive reinforcement, "The Best Quest".

In July, '93, I woke up one day, setting out for the third university. I arrived speaking with Mrs. Fore and she loved my idea "Challenged Conquistadors, Inc." & told me that Ms. Web was looking for someone to head up the Resource Department. Mrs. Fore also told me that the third university had a grant especially for an individual with a TBI. The grant was from the Foundation's primarily, with some local support, also. Remember that one foundation had fired me twice in '87, so I doubted my chances of getting it, because I had failed as a photographer & as an entrance/door greeter. They did not hold that against me or my Cognitive Challenges, then.

There were little funds, about $800 from the foundations, but I used what I had also because MAKING THE WORLD BETTER IS WHAT LIFE IS ALL ABOUT, ISN'T IT? Mrs. Fore at that time, now Dr. Fore, Ph.D., found an additional $500 dollars in January '94. The opportunity, CC, Inc., came to an end in the spring of May '94, officially, however I have never stopped because a dream is an opportunity! I surmised that teaching would be the best avenue to educate future adults to the reality that many cognitive challenges can be conquered. This was reinforced by the book: The Unschooled Mind, Gardner, 1991. Therefore, the third university knew of my Cognitive Challenges, because it was required by the foundations grant, before I started school there in the fall, '94. They allowed me to borrow money from the federal government for student loans, knowing that I may never work to pay the loans back, because they are still bugging me to pay the $250,000 back. I believe that I was created to activate, demonstrate, educate, initiate, motivate, stimulate, & validate all Challenged Conquistadors' individuals to do better than I have. I started taking classes to get my teaching certificate, Mrs. Fore, Mrs. George, & several others thought it was a great decision, since I focused on the linguistic intelligence (word smart). One of the multiple intelligences, Gardner spoke about in his book. The classes spanned five years. No one ever questioned my competency or even talked to me about my cognitive challenge affecting this decision concerning successfully teaching! As everyone saw I worked very hard promoting the cognitively challenged population. I was even noticed by some of the state's disability organizations as a powerful voice for the cognitively challenged community. I went to many support group's meetings, hospitals, & private individuals in communities that I heard about all over the state, visiting the cognitively challenged or not, demonstrating that the challenged can recover more than much in society, realize & some desire. Involvement with the Head Association lead to becoming involved with other organizations. Although none of these organizations ever considered me a successful candidate for employment, I've accomplished some success. A note; this year Dr. Advar, President, has informed me that it was my suggestion back at one of the conference meetings that has motivated her to try & get more positive media coverage for the cognitively challenged community. A fact is, if they do not see success then, they will not attempt to attain it. True or False? I believe that anyone can do anything they desire, because I am! I am not condemning anyone that is the way it is! Many people still refer to me as brain injured, afflicted, retarded, disabled, cripple, etc., i.e., terms in the disability environment/fear factor. Even when I applied for work with most of the organizations above they informed me that, I was brain disabled & couldn't do any job in their offices. Could this negative terminology, in itself, be discrimination? These are not favorable terms; our (humane) society has created to distinguish one human individual from another, especially since God created all humans in His eyes, perfect. What has happened to our compassion for one another, brotherly love, honorable, humane, considerate, caring, & correct behavior? It would look as if; we feed off others, who are thought of as inadequate/less as human, which also destroys our credibility. Almighty God had other plans.

It must be noted for the record that the loud music in the dorms & the cafeteria did contribute to an increase in cognitive challenges (episodes). Therefore, the third university did not meet my needs as a cognitively challenged student. The nurse & Disability Support Services (DSS) have records like me of the many visits to complain of this factor & its effects. I had to buy ear plugs to sleep. They worked some of the time, but not for all times, therefore I did badly on some exam's '94-'98. True, the correct medication wasn't discovered until May 2007, but the years from '78 or '81-'88 were especially difficult years in developing, especially with no attempt of correct medications. During these years, I took part in drinking alcohol activities, etc., therefore I eventually found myself on the streets, thus the medical care has been inadequate, especially

1986/1987. Even while on so-called correct medications many individuals wanted to institutionalize me, i.e., my mother (at age 12 in 1977), the state (1994-99), 2003, etc., but thanks to my wife this never happened. My wife, before we were married in 1999 was offered the position of Medicaid Waiver to take care of me, but she declined. I was never institutionalized by her, but I came close. She realized/convinced me that I didn't need to be institutionalized and I needed to be treated as a person able to take care of them self, independently. When one is treated as such, it is understandable why many give up. Miracles happen, when I met my wife. She could see my unique qualities under the imposed disability environment. As you can see from '78-'07 there was inadequate medical care, who was at fault? The medical profession doesn't really know the damage they do individuals, when they don't correctly diagnose individuals with correct diagnosis's/diseases. There were so many guesses about my condition from '78 up through '07.

I remember strongly being told I had Epilepsy, Schizophrenia, and Organic Brain Disorder with less than six months to live-this came as I was working on a Bachelor Degree at the second university, Alzheimer's disease, etc. These were Swift doctors' feelings. I was given a good brain & I would not accept being dehumanized like what was taking place in Swift. By this time, there had been many physicians, rehabilitation specialists, etc., involved with my care. I was visiting my physician in Flat, Dr. Fred's, MD, & she had some information on a physician in Memphis. Her name was Dr. May, MD, who is now in Boston according to Dr. Field, MD. Dr. May, MD, put me in the hands of Dr. Field, MD, who has done his best with me over the last 13 years to better my unique situation. He has always been behind my desire to teach. In fact, my desire to teach allowed Dr. Field, MD, some research. I'm doing things not done since 1977. However, if you talk to the Rehabilitative Service, they still feel I can't work or teach. It is a shame, when those entrusted with the fate of so many, act irresponsible. This is a tragedy & loss for us our world. The counselors told me to accept my brain injury as a final condition that wasn't rehabilitative.

With every new diagnosis came a new batch of drugs & the Rehabilitation system tried to convince me I belonged in a mental institution. They've been trying to convince me of this so called fact, even after the new drug has achieved such great results, etc.

Chapter Three

I was nominated and elected "GWCE Citizen of the Week" by third university. Third university's main focus for my program was the money, not human capabilities, that the foundations were distributing or why didn't they maintain what I initiated which is identical to Harvard ideas of "convincing models/positive role models" by Prof. Howard Gardner and "authoritative proof" by Prof. K. Egan. I started sending out information about my Quest, concerning speaking opportunities listed in "The Chronicle of Higher

Education" in '94-96. Also, remember they did not pay one penny to assist me in the speaking opportunities unless you feel they contributed through my disability check. Humans are never disabled, only their minds are led this way. These conference planners liked what God was doing through me; therefore I got many invitations to speak at several conferences. I never found a full-time sponsor. I paid for at least 94% of all the conferences, which I continued until my funds were depleted. Most of the funds came from the money I borrowed through federal grants for my teacher education degree. The third university encouraged me to use the funds for this educational purpose. A few of the conferences were international. The most important conference was the one in which (my program/paper: Challenged Conquistadors) were the lead presenter.

Conference was "Educators are Powerful," KCA Honor Society Conference. The paper demonstrates that cognitively challenged individuals can be productive, unlike the disability environment terminology that has been imposed/forced upon us. This is costing and who is responsible for this expense?

Since 1990-2000 was the decade of the brain, the number one disability in America, you would have thought that success, like mine would have been desired, because if no success is seen then it will not be duplicated. I was allowed at some of these public schools & colleges to, when volunteering for Students in Freedom to speak about stressing the importance of protecting the brain by wearing helmets while on bikes, etc.

Also, I need to tell you that I started watching a program on TV, because this program showed individuals dealing with challenges & conquering them. I wrote the executive director on July 10, '96, about showing Cognitive Challenged survivors successfully living & contributing to our society. His secretary, Julie in '96, called me a few days later to see, if I wanted a job or an episode on the issue. I stated an episode on Cognitive Challenge's conquering challenges & maintaining success. I did not take the job offer, I guess this was foolish. However, my goal is not fame or fortune, but to teach. However, during the month of September another program called "GC", portrayed an individual with a stroke. This individual suffered a lot of my similar challenges. This individual either was cut from the program or went onto other pursuits, because soon after the stroke he was gone. I was dishearten by this, because they didn't follow the line that an individual with Cognitive Challenge's can work their way back and be productive, like myself.   My seizures according to my doctor were positive, benign, & now I do not have them. Will this change employers perspective of me to enable me to work; it hasn't since 1996? Also, the third university is where I attended college but was denied an elementary teacher certificate, because they were scared of individuals like me, because of both my cognitive challenges on the non-accessible campus & my behavior from wrong medications, etc. This may be, because no one is educating them, that you can conquer these situations. Also, remember it cost you in taxes to support people like me, could not we achieve more by working together? Call me, when you are ready to start this change for the best (870)725-5119?

The third university denied me a teaching certificate, because I had an episode one morning in 1996. Remember that in '94, Mrs. Roy had sent Dr. Field, M.D., a letter to learn of my needed accommodations. However, in '97, the third university recommended me for a scholarship to teach from the State's Commission on People with Disabilities, which was reinforced by my successful completion of the State's Developmental Disabilities Planning Council and Family Leadership Training Project. There was another attempt to institutionalize myself in 1996. I have more than 10 years of higher education/college & it hasn't done me much good at getting a job. This nomination was by Dr. Smart, Ph.D., Professor of Education at the third university. I guess the third university felt that I was not teachable. They were in touch with my doctor to try different medications until one proved successful. Think of what I could have accomplished, if they had not had me on so much medication, perhaps the wrong one. After finishing the '96-'97 school year my GPA in Education Classes was 3.23 & overall 3.03 at the third university. Dr. Ray, Ph.D., who is Head of Students Enterprise (SE), told me that I couldn't participate in SE because of
the stink (accessibility) I had raised in the department of education. However, the previous two years I had been on the SE team and contributed to both of our victories. In fact, the year I was denied, the SE team did not win. Doesn't it make one wonder, why they can deny access then accept someone like myself? My presentation both years received standing ovations from the SE judges in '95 & '96. Also, the year before I joined SE, Dr. Ray's, Ph.D., daughter Julie was crowned Miss Cleveland, she became good friends with Miss Trout. Ms. Trout is challenged. I
assume he thought she would be a greater asset to our team?

Chapter Four

Below are the third university's officials' statements that are on tape that my spouse has also heard. Which were legal (Americans with Disabilities Act of 1990) to make, because my memory at that time was poor, because of the numerous drugs that I was taking. It would be during this time that family tried to institutionalize, myself. Dr. Pie, Ph.D., who is head of the special education department: "questioned the trauma for the kids 11/22-11/23/96", "you can't be put in a classroom"; "you're a threat & hazard 12/96-1/97"; "no one will hire you 1/11/97 by Forr, Ph.D., also"; "no education system is going to work/change to meet your needs because it would be foolish 1/16/97"; "you feel that the whole kindergarten program needs to be adjusted for your needs because you don't get enough rest"; "We've got to figure out a way to accommodate for the things...but didn't know how. 1/21/97"; "Too much hazard of being in class, until control by medicine"; "I did not possess skills to teach since I was disabled"; from this statement you can see that the third university didn't want to accommodate me since they had known about my CC since 1993. Dr. Token, Ph.D.: "Need to find program you can fit in"; "Your disability is a serious problem & no one will hire you"; "classroom isn't where you belong"; "If someone called me about you, I would have to say where problems exist, (remember that a company wanted to institutional me, again), & I couldn't perform"; "memory problems" 12/96-1/97". Dr. Smith, Ph.D.: "You can't move fast enough", "You can't keep up with 5 year olds" "I think a teacher aide position is obtainable". Dr. Cindy, Ph.D., told me "I could not be a counselor, because I must learn to overcome my disabilities," which was said in front of a class of hers. Mrs. Roy, (DSS), on August 5, '97, told me to accept the fact that I will not teach, which was before I had completed my second attempt like guaranteed by the USD of Education, D.M. Lee.

Mr. Took spoke with my professors in September of '97 about these statements & he told me that Dr. Pie, Ph.D., & Smith, Ph.D., stated "I cannot do the job" & on the second of September he called me into his office to tell me, which I already knew. This was more proof that the third university tried to disable me by establishing a negative educational self-fulfilling prophecy. On 7/31/98, Dr. Field, Ph.D., admitted he made a mistake with Diazepam, he said he would contact the university so they will not kick me out because it was not totally my fault for not learning. Therefore, it is possible that there were other opportunities of wrong medication & side effects which may have sedated me, which contributed to me being denied a teaching certificate, beside cognitive challenges created by falls.

In 1996: The Attorney General has a copy like AB Law firm dated August 18, '97: "The third university's position is based on observations (visual mental & physical skills only) of Mr. Best in a classroom setting." "Mr. Best was unable to successfully complete the practicum in which he was recently enrolled, and his professors do not believe that he can be successful in its elementary education program, especially in a situation like practice teaching, where he would have to manage a classroom full of children". "If you conclude that he is probably unlikely to successfully complete those tasks, the third university is prepared to negotiate a grade that will not cause him a problem in the future, if he will agree not to pursue a degree in elementary education at the third university". Another note, Mr. James, my attorney asked for punitive damages, which reinforces that he heard the professors on the tapes of mine!!!

It would be during these years of mental torture that the state again tried to confine my potential to an institution. There were two state employers, perhaps this is the reason the state didn't want me teaching? They tried to institutionalize me in group homes in both 1996 & 1999. This work of these has failed, because God is in control of my life.

Chapter Five

Then Mr. Sky called me in April, '00, to teach at Task Elementary School. I have taught successfully, for more than three weeks in April & May, 2000 & 1 day, in August, 2000, for Mr. Davis at Junior & Senior High School. Also, working was extremely delighting, because the store fired/forced me to quit, saying "They had to fire me, because I could not do the job". I've been tested & approved to teach at the vocational school. In fact, a number of the teachers were glad to have me, especially those who taught me, when I was in school before & after the accident. Also, there are a number of teachers from the third university at the schools. However, recently 11/30/00 Mrs. Raar informed me that I would not be called to teach because of my brain injury, she stated that "You can't handle the stress". Also, 1/10/01 I talked with Dr. Care, about why I had no job or teaching & she told me that since "the store had fired me & got me on disability, because I couldn't do the job, & no one else would hire me, either." I've worked 3 days teaching at Task Elementary School 3/01. I must keep pressing on for the day when all with cognitive challenges will be more productive than I. She didn't know that I was on the wrong drugs, while I was working at the store. I wonder how that I've achieved two degrees? It may be that she didn't like me or my behavior in high school, which possibly was due to not taking the medication that I had been placed on at Hospital in '78. My doctor stopped my medication in '79 & also the High School didn't continue giving me medicine. Talking about medications, since my wife expressed a concern that I was taking too much in regards to both lorazapam & risperdol, when we got together back in September 1999. I've been taken off both of these drugs & my life is much better. I have freedom, unlike before when I was drugged out. None of the schools in our area have asked me to substitute for them, until Vast called last week. You would think with a teacher shortage, a male elementary teacher could find work, especially in an elementary school, where positive male role models are needed especially for children without fathers. The schools that I'm registered with are several. I've been called to work one day by Cone Public Schools & this was back in August, '00 & 3 days in '01 at Vast Public Schools.

The university III, I spoke again with anyone about starting a chapter of "Challenged Conquistadors, Inc.", which I had been trying to initiate since 1993/1994. At first, I got the usual attitude "you are retarded & can do nothing" like I have for most of my life, especially from employers, which still happens today. I was finally, pointed to Dr. Dare, Ph.D., who after a few minutes he realized that what I was selling was exactly what they were trying to do with their TBI program. He asked me, if I would be interested in serving on their TBI Committee. I said yes. I must mention this fact, during the conversation I had an episode, which usually breaks my speech into fragments, however this day I was able to control enough that after the conversation, I asked Dr. Dare, Ph.D., if he noticed anything out of the ordinary. He replied, no. I stated with assertiveness, that I had an episode without him noticing. I was extremely proud of myself during that meeting. Again, who was in control; God!!

I've included some examples of learning experiences from my life: Wear helmets or Think First; Always turn a negative into a positive situation; can't never could do anything; people don't like to be classified;; as disabled; disabilities; challenges can be conquered; You can be whatever you want to be if you have God; No drugs or alcohol; Miracles happen; Don't be discouraged easily; Anything is possible.

Comments from elementary students: "It took a lot of courage for him to be what he is today. I learned that anyone can make the best out of a bad situation, no matter how bad it gets. I also learned that I probably shouldn't complain so much because there are people who have it a lot worse than I do." Many of the students said this: "I enjoyed the program". and "Good Luck
with your future plans". "I like everything that you said". "I would like for you to come back".

One foundation did try and employ me in the fall '99, but if they had hired me I would have had to work the third shift from 11 pm - 7 am. I could not work that shift, because I take medication to sleep at night. When I told them this, they said goodbye.

There are in excess of 1000 letters/faxes/emails of support that validates my brains' potential; another 566 Certified Sent Out Looking for Sponsorship/Work that were fruitless. This should remove all doubt, regarding my capabilities to do a job. My suicidal thoughts that were diminishing reappeared '96-'99 because the third university had me convinced that I could not teach, because of my cognitive challenge, but have almost became nonexistent, since I have started substitute teaching & volunteer teaching. My spouse, an intelligent person who married an individual like me, went with me to see my doctor January 18, '00. Dr. Field told us that I never had seizures, but what is called absence episodes that are momentary stares. Since he has had me believing that I have had seizures for over five years, I wonder if anyone will believe me, especially those whom I have been ostracized!

Well, I am being loved for the first time in my life & it is great. I believe my life has gone the way God desired, so that I can be a light in the darkness for others with cognitive challenges, because disabilities only diminish potential. These challenges have made me stronger, knowing that God will never leave a sinking ship, because He made all things perfect, the Best Quest! I was featured as "The Spirit of Swift". Therefore, this thinking had to be changed for the betterment of humanity. I knew better, because my father had conquered his challenges & I must do the same. I could be healed. I saw my mission in life was to promote that recovery from brain injury was achievable. My dreams of going to the Olympics & the US Air Force were derailed, because of the injury. I had started practicing for the Olympics as a driver, swimmer, etc., when I was 10 years old. I've always set my sights on these high prizes; however things changed when the accident occurred. I went from an "A" student to a "B" student, my physical strengths were less, and people perceived me as brain damaged which is still evident in Swift. I felt that the disabilities didn't matter, because as long as I could read, write, spell, etc., I had just as much chance of succeeding as the next individual. I was wrong.

Chapter Six

Parents like mine need to be punished! Sincerely, I was created to benefit the entire human population by positively activating, demonstrating, educating, initiating, motivating, stimulating & validating all minds to conquer CC, since it is the #1 challenger or disabler in America among children and injury of the current wars, with one happening every 18.5 seconds, please do not let it happen to you. There are few future adult/children models of success, so what will you do, when it happens to you? In fact, the cost last year was $2.3 billion, 2010, because youth were not wearing helmets. In fact, cognitive challenges are the number one disabler in America among youth. We must change this!

I have, also, been nominated for Use Your Life Award from the Oprah Winfrey Show.

A quote from the Native Auto-Biographical Institute on nominates "Selection is based entirely upon merit, and I congratulate you, Mr. Best, on the fine example you are setting for your peers and society." which I did obtain." I must be doing something right!

My efforts are finally reaping the benefits that many have said would never be achieved. If I would have followed the lead of nurses & other Cognitively Challenged care givers, I would have never made it to where I am today; I would've been convinced that I was disabled & useless. The reason is many hospitals treat us as helpless, which I have never been beside the 5 months of hospitalization from September 25, 1977-March 10, 1978. Many individuals with challenges believe they are entitled to special assistance, because of their condition; well I did not have any assistance. I am neither angry nor boasting, but if I can achieve success, should not we try & inspire others with Cognitive Challenges, especially, to do their best?

Defamation is false charges maliciously calculated to damage another's reputation, i.e., disabled, disadvantaged, handicap, cripple, etc. On judgment day, God will not be able to hold me accountable or responsible for these crimes of indecency. Have a Best Day!! Another fact that may seem strange is Mrs. Fore asked me to record my daily activities in '93 & I did not quit until '98.

I sure am glad I have all of this documented for proof! I have beaten the test by being my best, no or yes? Others with cognitive

challenges need to see success, before they will believe/attempt
challenging obstacles. The cognitively challenged need to know that
they are taken seriously,
especially when all of society feels you are a liability. Many
individuals suffer from Post-Traumatic Stress Disorder (PTSD),
however I also conquered this adversary.

My poems: Reasons, Realizations, Journey, & Puppets on a String.

"Reasons"

Sometimes we think,

Sometimes we drink,

Sometimes our mind,

Is lost in liquor or wine!

The trouble between both black & white,

Is that each see their view as right!

Let's work together for a single master,

Instead of fighting which ends in disaster.

We could try annihilation of others,

But I ask you who would go first?

With so much deviance in our behavior,

The human race is quickly becoming a disgrace!

With more and more conflict, prejudice, and discrimination,

What is becoming of our so-called wonderful nation?

It is not too late for us to live in assimilation,

But the longer it is put off, this leads to disorganized nations!

All of us have God given rights,

Why can't we live together peacefully and quiet?

Let's all work together and end this vicious cycle,

Let's stop xenophobia before it destroys us!!!!

"Realizations"

There was a boy, Who played all day.

His name was Jam, He laughed all the way.

Sometimes sad, But others glad.

Sometimes he had, But was very mad.

Until he viewed, A young man stealing a toy.

Jam spoke aloud,

Yelling come play with me, Young man.

The young man stopped on a dime,

Could he believe his ears this time?

Someone to play with at last,

Jam inquired his name.

Peanut Butter he exclaimed,

They got together; Their differences caused a change.

Which was great this showed their intelligence!

Jam had found a friend,

From desiring a toy, But realized a greater joy!

Thus Peanut Butter & Jam got along just fine,

They learned that others joys can be others toys!!

"Journey"

Down,

Up!

What can be expected?

Not much!

If you do not jump,

We can all see limitations!

But the Master can create innovations,

Not the popular way!

But there is a way,

Nothing can be achieved,

As long, as you are deceived!

Far from this road shall I travel,

Where all my riches shall unravel!

Something can be said for uniqueness,

It creates oneness!

Often in those joyful times of youth,

I sought not the advice of elders.

But rather choose my own ways,

Which challenged with greater difficulty my days!

One can learn, but a price must be paid,

Will it be stop and listen or wish and mourn!

Life is great, but do not make this mistake,

Take your life for another's sake!

"Puppets On a String!"

Is it a state of confusion or unlimited knowledge?

Where are we all to go?

When one is down and beat,

Why do we allow?

Many questions, which have been asked before.

The common resolution is one must persevere!

There are many paths to take or not.

What is the loss, if one takes no risk?

There is a method, which is sure to complete.

This approach is often ill fated.

This question remains.

What is the euphoria of the misery?

What must one do to realize their fate?

Results are so inestimable, but risk is so extraordinary!!

What will you do?

Be a puppet or an innovator like I?

"A Challenged Conquistador!"

Risk takers Can be Winners!!

LIFE IS RISK!

No Question, No Rewards!

Nothing!!

I hopefully will be believed, which will encourage others with
cognitive challenges to succeed in life, because they may be able.
Jesus Christ died for us are we any better than too
sacrifice for Him?

I would like you to know that I'm finishing college to teach
students in both preschool & elementary school, but this failed,
because I couldn't complete College Algebra, a fourth time. I've
been attempting this feat for the last 16 years in Swift, thus my

experiences are critical for others to succeed. It is my sincere
desire to teach all students that they can conquer many of the
adversaries/challenges/disabilities/differences they confront during
life, because we all will face challenges of some type, therefore
our positive reaction should be natural. The new medications
(Lamictal) that I'm now taking today is allowing me to do things not
done in 30 years & Invega, is demonstrating more miracles, along
with Excelon Patches. If you know of any
speaking opportunities that exist, please utilize my recovery. We
all model someone; therefore more can succeed, when our success is
seen as natural. It may seem difficult, but it is attainable.

It has been realized that I can teach, because I've taught for ABC
USA for over a 150 days. This is the realization of my human
potential. The troubling evidence is all state organizations seem
to feel that I'm not intelligent, however the state spent millions
to save me? Could this be a conspiracy?

To end with I've included some quotes from teachers & students of my
recovered state: The following are also concerns of mine with regard
to the cases; witnesses of cognitive skills to do the job are X, Y,
etc., who called me to work between 100-150 days to substitute: She
stated that "I was one of their most demanded substitutes" & "a
positive role model"; "was glad they sent me, she told me that they
trust & respect me, 1.29.09." "stated I was part of teaching team,
1.23.09." "told student that I was a teacher & to do what I said,
1.23.09." "told me "I did a good job with children, 1.21.09." "One
teacher told me I was the best with class because of several trouble
makers & the last 2 subs walked out on them. At the end of the day,
I was asked how I liked subbing them, said great, & the teacher said
from now on when misses, we'll ask for you., 1.6.09." "Principal
requested for me to teach for again, 12.11.08." "said it was good
for me to be there, 12.11.08." "stated "I impressed principal with
orderly control of problem students., 10.14.08" "Told by one
teacher that I'm very calm with children., 10.10.08." "contacted to
start teaching for them, 10.8.08." "I was asked by the teachers at
the if I could teach again tomorrow for but I told them - Wed. is
taken by the, They said they need someone for
Fri Afternoon. "was relieved to learn that I would be teaching
tomorrow., 9.29.08." "Called by one teacher I was good male role
model." 9.19.08." "I was doing a good job with teaching.,
8.22.08". Substitute taught in for 8.12.08 & 8.13.08.", "It is hard
to find good subs". Another teacher who went to school with me at
university where they denied me a teaching certificate
because of brain injuries on campus - stated "good job on handling
those fifth graders in PE the other day." One teacher at called me
a brave soul" in regards to teaching fifth graders., 5.14.08". "I
was a good teacher & handled class well, 4.18.08. One teacher at
stated "it is good to see you here today", 4.10.08. "asked if I
wanted to work tomorrow", 3.5.08. "Will see you next year-
teaching", teacher stated.

Quotations from students: Learning measured 4/12/95 School,
Arkansas, 6th Grade: 1) "Today I've learned that miracles can

happen. Even if doctors or other experts say you cannot recover it is still possible, if you try hard enough. No matter how hard family, friends, & others get down on you if you want if you can accomplish it. Christian H.; 2) 1) I've learned a lot of people's problems are worst than mine & can be overcame. 2) I've learned how it feels for a person to be ridiculed and laughed at. 3) I've learned that with the help of the lord all of life's trials can be overcame, but you have to try. 4) I've learned about some of the terms often used to set aside & discriminate and how demeaning they are. Leah S."; 3) I learned that you can change a negative situation into a positive situation. You should wear helmets to protect your head. You can be whatever you want to be, if you have God. And you should be careful when playing football, ice hockey, etc. Latoya S.; 4) Be careful when playing sports. 2) Call 911 when something goes wrong. 3) Challenged people can do amazing things. 4) Can't never amounted to anything. 5) DON'T GIVE UP. 6) Always believe in yourself. No matter what anyone says. 7) You self-esteem is the most important thing to you. 8) People don't like to be classified as disabled. Tami H.; 5)Today, I have learned that our lives are valuable and they can be easily taken away. There are choses (choices) like drugs and some very dangerous sports and alcohol & everyone just needs to learn to say NO to all of the life taking things in the world. We have to set an example by making a better future for others, lets start today by being accountable. Stephanie B.; 6) I've learned that by having determination and a strong will you can achieve anything, such as living through a number of head injuries & educating yourself to your fullest potential, by having a will to learn. I've also learned that I should respect those who are called "disable" more. Gwendy W.; 7) Today I learned that Football is one of the leading causes of head injuries. I learn that you need to trust in Jesus, cause miracles really can happen, & I learned that you don't need Drugs & Alcohol to solve a problem. It don't Matter who doubts you, all you got to do is believe in yourself! Jamell B. S.; 8) That you can do whatever you want if you want to do it. Making things positive when they are really negative also being caution doing what you like to do and be smart playing about it. You did Great! Katherine O.; 9) I learned about I do anything I want be in life only if I work hard to be it. I learn that my head is the most important thing on the body. James J.; 10) Today I learned that anybody can be somebody if they want it bad enough. Try not to be discouraged if something bad happens to you. Just face it, and believe in yourself. Make the worst things to the best things. Everybody have their own potential. Joe T.; 11) I've learned that you can turn a bad situation into something good by working hard & believing in yourself. You can also prevent a bad situation from happening by avoiding drugs & being careful with your life. I enjoyed the program & Good Luck with your future plans. Ashley N.; 12) 1) You can do anything if you try hard enough. 2) No one is a nobody! 3) Be careful at what you do because bad things can also happen to anyone. 4) Don't mess up you life with drugs. 5) Be all you can be. Courtney R.; 13) 1) You can do anything you set your mind to. 2) Make the best of any situation. 3) Don't let anyone look down on you & your as good as you think you are!! 4) Be Careful! Sally S.;

14) Today I have learned that life is very valuable & precious. Don't do drugs because they don't accomplish anything and if you want to be something Bad enough you'll work hard at it & be very successful. April T.; 15) Learned about a man who had open-heart surgery at the age of 4. he was also hit by a 18-wheeler. His parents and family members didn't like him & treated him like he was a girl. He worked hard to become where he is today. He has experienced a lot of things during his lifetime. His story was very very sad. It took a lot of courage for him to be what he is today. No Name; 16) I learned that anyone can make the best out of a bad situation, no matter how bad it gets. I also learned that I probably shouldn't complain so much because there are people who have it a lot worse than I do. I also plan to learn what epilepsy is, and how to deal with a situation that is potentially dangerous. Leslie C.; 17) I've learned about brain injuries and how people will treat you when you have a brain injury. Wear helmets don't lay them on the ground wear them. Thanks for coming I liked everything that you said. I would like for you to come back! Latonya E.; 18) That be careful about what you do. 2) You can be all that you can be. 3) Try harder to improvement & you'll make it. 4) Don't do drugs unless you have to. 5) Life isn't a joke it's reality. Natasha K.; 19) I learned that anything is possible if you work at it but, not overnight. Football is the number two sport that causes head injuries with a helmet. Blake S."

College Program: The speech today inspired me. It showed me that if you set your mine & are optimistic all things are possible. The speech was inspirational in that it inspired me to have a more positive attitude. All people should be given a chance to accomplish anything. This country is supposed to be The Land of Opportunity. I'm glad to see that people that have been in life altering accidents don't just sit around and let it consume the rest of their lives. I think there should be more positive people in the world like our speaker because the world will be a better place. I feel that this presentation gave our class a positive image. Your story has touched all of our hearts. I believe people with cognitive challenges are still human. They need assistance and special needs to help improve their everyday life. It is worth the effort to try to improve their lifestyle quality to lead them to be a better citizen and prospective life. I have a cousin that is a TBI Survivor. He was six years old when he received the injury. He was told that he will never be able to walk, talk, or anything. He overcame his illness and is now a Christian speaker. Her reeds on a 7 year old level, but can tell you anything you want to know about the Bible. I am glad to see that you are able to do so much! You are an inspiration! I think that after today my perception of cognitively disabled people have changed for the good. My perception of those with cognitive challenges has changed from the speech today. I used to see patients in the hospital with a coma, and find it hard to believe that they would recover. Now, I have more hope. I have a more positive attitude of those who are challenged. It has further inspired me to want to work with these individuals. I feel that those with cognitive impairments are just like everyone else they just need special help in certain area's.

Today I have realized that this can not hinder those who feel strongly about something. I believe those with cognitive challenges are people too & should be treated & respected just like everyone else. Just because there is some sort of disability involved doesn't exempt them from being treated as equals. "I didn't know someone could sustain 41 brain injuries & still function & communicate as well as you. You are an inspiration & I wish you luck in all you do. God Bless You!" "I learned that with a positive attitude you can do anything! Thank you for speaking!" "I learned that attitude & faith really can make a miraculous difference in recovery after a brain injury. Also, I didn't realize that "cognitive challenge" was a preferred term among brain injury survivors. Now that I'm aware of that I'll be more mindful so I ensure the respect of people w/ brain injuries." "I learned that keeping a positive outlook on the situation is important. Even though he was faced with obstacles and challenges he was able to overcome them through faith & optimism. I thought his experience was motivational and inspiring." "The use of negative labels are challenging to the survivors of brain injury. Positive connotation of the label cognitively challenged is better. Positive psychology reflects better outlook on life." "A person needs determination, perseverance, & humor to help recover." "I learned the negative impact that negative terms can have on a person's life a feeling of self-worth. Also, I have very happy to see the progress that a person in your situation has the potential to make. Your talk was very informative for all people." "Shawn knowledgably presented many information thoughts. I learned about the importance of wearing a helmet. I also learned about the negative aspects of the labels on cognitively challenged persons. He informed us about concussions & many other aspects of brain injury." "I learned that having a positive attitude is important factor in people with brain injury. And that it is important to find purpose in helping others who have also sustained in brain injury." "Positive terms are key to outlook & psychological health! Advocating for positive association of terms with previously negative views can make a huge difference." "He is trying to get rid of the negative aspects of brain injuries and focus on the positive. Get rid of retarded, disabled, and handicapped. If you think of things optimistically, you are more likely to succeed.

Wear a helmet!' "I learned to always stay positive about life no matter what challenges I face to ALWAYS wear a helmet!" "I learned that as an occupational therapist when working with clients who have cognitive challenges, that encouraging a positive outlook is incredibly important. Encouraging each client to focus on what they are able to do is important." "Sean-His work is endorsed by Dr. Poussaint from Harvard. The use of positive terms such as "cognitively challenged, can promote increased healing. Common problems: fear, memory, anxiety, siting, drinking, paranoid, axtaia, emotional control, etc." "Terms such as handicapped and disabled can be very offensive to an individual with a brain injury. Also, many employers are hesitant on hiring an employee with multiple falls on the." "Always wear a helmet. Positive outlook, self-respect is ultimately very important; you can help others by informing them of reality of cognitive challenges."

"Positive outlook". "I learned about the challenges you face every day. Some of the challenges you face is being called negative words, poor balance, falling sometimes, and sometimes emotion is hard to handle. As occupational therapist we always need to look at the positive for a client. Never be negative and say you can't do anything." " I learned that you need to have a positive outlook on life. To be more careful and to be respectful to those that have experienced brain injury." "I thought it was very interesting and impresive that you have advocacted to change the terminology and reduce the negative connotations. Thank you very much for all your work!" "To be more careful w/ the words disabled & handicapped-and to keep an optimistic outlook." "I learned that a positive attitude, perseverance, and constant faith can help you through any situation. I learned to be grateful of my situation and to always try to better myself." "I learned to label people positively. Keep up the good work!" "I learned a lot about how the community treats victims of brain injuries. It was very neat to hear how successful he has become politically. I am so glad to have met him today. He is so positive and it make so glad that he is here w/ us." "I learned about the importance of positive thinking in recovery and to be careful with the use of negative terms." "I learned the significance that is attached to various "disability" terms and effect their negativity can have. I also saw first-hand the effect of motivational/positive attitude." "You cannot file a discrimination lawsuit be you are considered incompetent." "Always use respectful language when referring to disabilities." "To say cognitive disability instead retarded or mentally handicapped. The power of having a positive atttitude & how that can help you have a faster and more complete recovery than just having a negative attitude." "I learned that the power of positive thinking is very strong and that multiple brain injuries can be overcome." "Must have self-respect to project it. Do not file a discrimination lawsuit; the judge will not pay you any mind. They fired you for the kids not respecting you-Shocking!" "I really appreciated you being here. I glad to see someone like you who has come so far in your recovery. Keep going and never stop!" "Motivation and determination are necessary to succeed through life. Terms like disabled, handicapped, and retarded are negative to both the person being called them and society in general." "I learned that many of the terms and words we use can actually hinder our clients." "I learned about the dangers of concussions. Positive thinking is extremely important." "I learned that the proper term for brain injury is cognitive challenge." "I learned about psychoneuroimmunology and how the patient's psychological state can affect an immune system. I found it to be very inspiring story and really believe in a positive attitude getting you far in the recovery process." "I learned about the negativity that some popular terms such as "handicapped" can convey to a person who is affected by a disease or disorder." "Use the term cognitive challenge instead of disability or brain injury, bicycle safety is key-wear helmet, psychoneuroimmunology - power of positive/optimist thinking to influence health, medications can be good or bad."

Below are many statements that were exchanged between me & my instructors at the third university with dates: (I was told by Mrs. Fore, Ph.D., to keep records of all situations/conversations for the Foundations):

However first, I think you should know what my physician told SU: Dr. Field, M.D., Ph.D.. Dr. Field, MD, Ph.D., has been my physician since 1992. The following is information shared with the third university with dates. I'd like you to know that Dr. Field, MD, Ph.D., worked at Harvard for five years & spent fifteen years at John Hopkins Hospital. His specialty is epilepsy. He stated for the record: December 6, 1994, Dr. Field, MD, PhD. "In 1977, Shaun Best had suffered a significant head injury with three (3) months of coma." "Please note than seizure-like (but non-epileptic) spells are part & parcel of his posttraumatic state." June 6, 1996, "Shaun's seizures are of a minor type, he never hurts himself, and he regains awareness within 1-2 minutes. They require no particular intervention and are of a benign type." May 2, 1997, Dr. Field, MD, Ph.D., "....he has startle attacks....which present no danger to himself or others, & followed by quick recovery." "I am very concerned if this basically benign handicap is considered a hindrance to his academic progress." Dr. Field, MD, was in constant communication with SU from the start of my education from 1994-1999 on these dates in particular 12.6.94, 6.6.96, 5.2.97, etc. October 1, 1996 Roy is writing Dr. Field, MD, to find out more about me for their information (accommodations needed). October 9, 1996 Dr. Ray, Ph.D., about being on the SU Students Enterprise (SE) team, "he doesn't want me on it because of the stink that I've caused in the education department". I assisted in winning two prior SE Awards in 1995 & 1996.October 11, 1996 this was the first day that I've been spoken to regarding my "The Challenged Conquistadors" shirt, after incorporation in SWIFT, 6.2.95. Accordingly, "the shirt perpetuates (lasts indefinitely) a perceived conflict of interest", stated Dr. Pie, Ph.D., which was written on a piece of paper, her handwriting, I possess this document.

November 22/23, 1996 I told the teachers about my fall. Dr. Pie, Ph.D., and Dr. A. Smith, Ph.D., acted very funny today, since I told them about the accident, "telling me that I would have to have 100% control", they've known that is unlikely. Then they "questioned the trauma the children would suffer", also telling me that "I couldn't be put in classroom, because I didn't know when one will occur, and that I'm responsible for this"; "what if this had happened in a classroom & how would you explain it to the students". No brain scans were done to determine whether it was a seizure or a loss of balance. They sounded like excluding me as a result of this one bad spell, brain scans can be ran and determine whether I had a seizure or a loss of balance. Dr. Pie, Ph.D., "needs to hear from Field, so I called to tell him to make contact or they will kick me out of the program". The third university had a nurse & could have run an MRI to determine whose fault it was. Then, Dr. Field, MD, did not call

me back to say he had called Dr. Pie, Ph.D., about medication. November 26-27,
1996 Dr. Field called about my brain, "added medication which could have contributed to me not successfully completing tasks", etc. He is going to give me another drug to offset my challenges. I worked on the papers for SE competition. I called the third university nurse about his calling, she wanted to know what triggered the seizure, I told him that the stress of being at this school and the battles of this environment, inclusion, teachers, etc. I went to the nurse who checked my blood pressure and it is OK.

In November/December of 1996 I called the SU nurse about Dr. Field, MD, calling; Dr. Pie, PhD, stated, "wanted to know what triggered the seizure", January 10, 1997, Dr. Pie, Ph.D., "told me that I did not progress as fast as I should have remarking that when she sat in on one event when I was changing the letters or numbers of the days of the month, I said you saw the challenge, how can I correct it by allowing a student to do it for me". Dr. Pie, Ph.D., "praised my notes of Ms. Falls' work with the students and asked my permission to share them visually with Ms. Fall, I said great, teamwork". I asked Dr. Pie, Ph.D., "about why I got the I's and she told me again that "I was not adequately prepared to teach 0-7, she suggested 7-15 or 16". Which I'm teaching today. January 11, 1997, Today both Dr. Pie, Ph.D., and Dr. Forr, Ph.D., said "that no school will hire me"! I felt ashamed & stupid for investing time & money to teach & being denied. January 14, 1997, Dr. Pie, Ph.D., stated "that I did not join the team or act as a team player in regard to class assignments!" Dr. Field, MD, is yet to answer Mrs. Roy about accommodations, adequately! I had no other student to team with, but an experienced teacher, since this had not been done before (first time), therefore I had no path/pattern to follow. Remember that a student with a head injury had attempted the education program & failed before I started in 1994. Thus the difficulty of this situation was apparent. How could I do teamwork with an experienced teacher, unlike the other teams of student teachers in the learning process/discovery? I told her about my situations with females, and that I keep it professional Now she knows why I did not engage with them. She said the other 22 students were able to do this and why you weren't able, they never asked or told me of working together. The trauma from Drs. Pie and Smith, Ph.D.'s last semester caused the bad grades to drop below a 3.0 GPA. Also, the noise in the cafeteria may have contributed. Quick change is a must in life. Teamwork! On January 15, 1997, As I talked with Dr. Who, Ph.D., about my classes, "he said go and ask Dr. Forr if you make A's and B's this semester are you going to allow me to student teach". On January 16, 1997, Dr. Pie, Ph.D., said to me "no education system is going to work/change to meet your needs because it would be foolish". On January 21, 1997, Dr. Pie, Ph.D. stated "you feel that the whole kindergarten program needs to be adjusted for your need"; I've been excluded", "not necessarily, we've got to figure out a way to accommodate" (Did the third university do this?) this should have been done day 1, not half way through the year, this is not my responsibility but the educators (Isn't our future at stake?);" "teacher skills which are not textbook; has nothing to do with personally; transition songs, finger plays for keeping quiet (Disability Support Services never helped me to learn these or suggested ways to learn them, therefore no accommodations); when working with children and must recognize it"; want to for the record or quote some of what I recorded on my tape for further reference with Dr. Pie, Ph.D., "we are going to talk when Dr. A. Smith, Ph.D., when she gets back, gets back; the sentences devastated me; her standards at the risk of my health; "I've been excluded", Dr. Pie, Ph.D., I did not make this goal & Pie, Ph.D., "wants ways that I can conquer this challenge"; more than observer, which can be documented by my earlier classes? I was never encouraged by any to interact with children as a class, but as small units; who did not involve themselves because no formal invitation, which (Dr. Pie, Ph.D., said is natural because the others did and you did not; I had the wrong mind set of observing and not participating with others;} I've never been around young people; we can not change a whole program for you; I am reserved; what can we do to help you? Dr. Pie stated; & the girls never said anything as team work; "The assignment: experiences and what you did and didn't do" from Dr. Pie, Ph.D. Why was I abandoned by the third university, no guidance or accommodations? January 25, 1997, Dr. Forr, Ph.D., said "we never guaranteed you a job". July 1, 1997, Dr. Cindy, Ph.D., informed me that "I could not become a counselor because I must learn to overcome my disabilities". August 5, 1997, Ms. Roy said "for me to accept the facts that you will not teach". This was said before my second attempt was completed. September 2, 1997, Mr. Took of Student Affairs did some background work to see if what I said was true. His first answer was Pie & Dr. A. Smith say "you can't do the job", second response was "more paper work needed to be done", etc.

These are recordings of some conversations, because I had to keep a recorder with me to remember their requests & ADA states school has a copy: On Audio Tapes: December 1996-January 1997: Tape 1: Dr. Pie, Ph.D., "How do we accommodate?" "You are a hazard & threat; you should never be in a classroom". "No one will hire you because of your disability". Dr. A. Smith, Ph.D., "I'll try to get the administration to buy into a withdrawal". Mr. Token, Ph.D., "Your disability is a serious problem & no one will hire!" Tape 2: Mr. Token, Ph.D., "nothing in writing/reason for I's & memory problem & no school will hire." Tape 2B: Dr. Pie, Ph.D. "You believe that the whole kindergarten program should be adjusted because you don't get enough rest. How do we change what we except for the program? What are you asking for? We've got to figure out how to accommodate for the things..." Dr. A. Smith, Ph.D., "You are liable for a lot of things. Figure out what to do. You can't move fast enough." "I've watched you grow & I think a teacher aide position is obtainable, not a lot of liability." Dr. Pie, Ph.D., stated "too much of a hazard of being in class, until controlled by medication". Dr. A. Smith, Ph.D., stated "you can't keep up with 5 year olds". Mr. Token, & Dr. Pie, Ph.D., stated "no one will hire". Mr. Token, stated "many problems like memory", "classroom isn't where you belong" & "no school will hire." Dr. Roy, Ph.D., stated "couldn't

make certificate accessible for only one, there had to be more."
Dr. Roy, Ph.D., like Dr. Ray, Ph.D., "a money issue". The third
university never consulted Dr. Field, MD, PhD., in '96 about
medication changes to control my seizures better, or not to my
knowledge, or Mr. Roy (Student Support Services) never contacted to
see what he (Dr. Field, MD, PhD,) said or suggested. Remember that
Dr. Pie, Ph.D., asked me "how to accommodate, wasn't this the job of
Mrs. Green, Disability Support Services"? Why do I have these
recordings, if the teachers at SAU never denied me a teaching
certificate? What do these statements refer to if not exclusion? I
have the cassettes for proof.

The third university School of Education nominated me for a teaching
certificate from the Jam Governor's Commission on People with
Disabilities in 1997. The third university Professor Emeritus of
Psychology and Counseling, wrote an article; SHARING: The article
title: "Transformation of Handicaps to Challenges" where she
referenced my work to the book: The Unschooled Mind, 1991, H.
Gardner. As you can see, making the third university comply with
the ADA did me great harm along with the 20 plus head injuries on
the campus, however it insured millions of dollars to the third
university for compliance. Could this be the reason? The state has
denied me a teaching certificate for the last 15 years, blackballed?
I left the third university in 1999, because they felt I needed to
be institutionalized. This is where I meet up with my wife who
convinced me I was competent, even though Hash had tried to
convince, my girlfriend at that time felt that I was incompetent..
By Mr. Hash employing her to take care of me, (Medicaid Wavier '99),
it served him in neglecting my potential. I've started 5.06
attending fourth university, where they feel I can teach. What is
so funny or odd is the first university allowed me to complete a
degree in 1985 & in 1997 the main campus of third university didn't.

One reason for their denial could be the number of head injuries
between 1993 and 1997. I had other concussion's: 10.6.94 I fell at
SAU; 3.13.95, balance issues/psychomotor seizure, fell on right
shoulder at third university/non-accessible steps; fell 3.20.95,
balance issues on unleveled ground; 3.21.95 (2), Graham Annex is
non-accessible and I have fell twice (unleveled ground) and sprang
my ankle; 3.30.95, fell on stairs from seizure jerk; 6.4.95, fell on
steps from seizure jerk; 7.6.95 hurt head from fall - dance class;
Made a statement to Mike & Sam: 7.28.95 that I did not dress up a
lot was because I trip and tear clothes & shoes up, in addition to
seizures; 8.12.95 need rails for showers, because of slipping &
fall; 8.15.95 I left the business building my legs locked due to
seizures and I fell in front of the highway on my hands; 9.4.95 fell
in shower hurting back & jarring head (whip-lash movement),; 2.5.96
slip & fall (ice) Dr. Ray's; 2.16.96 (2) two falls from not enough
rest & noise in cafeteria; slip & fall in Food Management Cafeteria
& fall on track; 11.22.96, fell from seizure-kept apologizing;
documented by RA, Joe Smith; cut face; hit head on computer monitor;
threats while in TV room; brain swelling saw nurse 11.26.96 or;
1.9.96/7, fell on right shoulder in Talbot hall, where Maintenance
men saw and reported; 6.1.96/7, fell on steps-seizure jerk;

9.19.96/7, seizure almost busting head, jerking; 9.21.96/7 (2), fell in room due to loud music in early morning hours hit face on computer monitor/bled (cut under eye) at SAU; (2) 10.18.96/7 & 12.18.96/7 fell down non-accessible steps at one level was railed and one level wasn't railed-fell on both; Dean of Student Life Center medicated since nurse was out; shoulder, neck, brain are hurting; head still hurting 12.19-21-96/7; 6.19.96/7, (2) fell on railed steps & non-railed steps, two levels of steps at Curriculum Center; 6.8.98, seizure & jarred head on fall to ground; 7.6.98, fell and broke skin on fore head from fall, etc. These falls at SU has resulted in these additional falls: 7.21.03 fell backwards at FC, (Work); 8.11.03 fall at FC, icebox entrance; 10.13.03 fall & hit right side of head, FC; 1.8.04 (2) fell walking on cardboard boxes & fell at trashcans, FC; 2.26.04 someone at work hit me in the back of the head at FC, but unintentional; 6.9.05;(4) 8.16.05, 1.31.06, & 2.21.06 falls at Natural Plaza (Work); 11.27.06 seizure/fall at home; 2.10.09 fall at work Band Stand; 7.2.09 fall at home because too drunk from legal drugs Dr. Jod gave for anxiety; 9.11.09 fall at Castle; 4.8.11, fall at gas station hitting head.

The university documented several injuries. They claimed they were not at fault. A final thought on my third university experience; I continued conducting research on the perspective of individuals with challenges vs. individuals with head injury/disabilities as started at the second university in 1992.

Individuals with disabilities, whether it be cognitive, physical, visual, etc., imposes a negative on an individual's potential, whereas if an individual is addressed in a neural or beneficial capacity such as challenged, then there is not a negative perspective, i.e., disabled, handicapped, etc., to conquer. The resulting organization, "Challenged Conquistadors, Inc." was nationally & internationally recognized for our positive perspective, which enhanced our awareness in schools. This program was developed for our youth who are more adaptive to change/differences. There were many speaking events: Pa Ta Pi Honor Society; ABC Learning Institute; Retention Strategies; Global Communication; Applied Ethics; Diversity; etc.

When I lived on the streets back in the late 80's, life was especially tough, since survival is difficult for the so-called normal; the challenged have been treated as non-normal/disabled. Life can be enhanced with a positive perspective of oneself. Here are comments that I've heard, regarding teaching. Check them out for yourself, check phone records, etc. November 28, 2000, Mrs. Raar, stated, "I couldn't handle any class of students." January 10, 2001, Mrs. Care stated, "The Store proved you were brain disabled & it would be foolish if anyone hired you to teach", also of Vast. As Mrs. Care stated "can't you realize that your brain is disabled." A few days earlier she (Mrs. Care) had just presented me with a certificate from Vast Center passing their requirements to teach in the public schools, which I possess, a copy.

August 30, 2001 I contacted Mr. Tally at the request/instructed by Mr. Tally about the Provisional Licensure Program to teach school/finish the teaching program. Mr. Tally signed the professional licensure form to allow me to complete my certification at Vast Public Schools, which I possess, a copy. On October 4-5, 2001 Dr. Petty stated "that he would make calls to local superintendents for me to get teaching jobs". What happened between June 2001 & today, especially since I passed the substitute teacher test in Vast in August 2000 & Smoke Substitute Teacher requirements October 10/4-5/2001. In early 2002, Mr. Tally of Department of Education stated "going to do away with teacher certification". March 12, 2002 (#8-Email) I had a scheduled interview with Mr. Spirit, 9:30 am Tuesday March 12, 2002. Why did Mr. Spirit state "that individual schools have the right to deny anyone/someone a degree/teaching certificate" & why didn't university in '85 or second university in '93 do this? Mr. Thought, I'm waiting on the responses to the letter I sent you on the 11th. Thank You. Is it true to assume that you don't need teachers?

COPY OF THE LETTER I LEFT AT YOUR OFFICE   Mr. Petty, superintendent, Smoke Schools asked me to ask you some of these questions. 1) If I have Special Education (SE) hours can I then, get NTTLP & teach SE, since shortage? 2) Why wasn't I allowed to start NTTLP last year, when Mr. Can? Mr. Can told me I had the job, if you allowed me into the program & I had the scores from the third university. My Computer based/Accommodations Praxis/Pre-Professional Skills Test (PPST) Scores needed in 1996, which I passed: Reading 316; Writing 174; Math 322. 3) Will I be allowed to teach in either/or public /private schools? It cost money driving to these schools with this information, when you're not employed. 4) Why did you (state department) tell me no school would hire me, due to my seizures, but if you check my records, I've never had epileptic seizures, but rather non-epileptic spells/episodes, which pose no threat or danger to anyone? The third university has the documentation, like I do, dated 12/6/94 & 5/2/97 from Dr.
Field, Harvard Alumni. 5) Why did the professors at the third university say the harsh things (you're a threat, hazard, dangerous to the students, very risky for you to be in classroom, don't know when one will happen, great liability to the school) they did & do they still do it to others who are recruited/enrolled to be teachers on state sponsored education, etc.? 6) Why didn't the third university suggest Non-Traditional Teacher Licensure Program (NTTLP), if they thought I could teach in 1997? March 12, 2002 (#8-Email) Mr. Take: I had a scheduled for you an "interview with Mr. Spirit, 9:30 am Tuesday (#14-Email) Mrs. Fred states "Mr. Thought got your email and asked me to check with you and get an update on your situation. He was concerned about you. We went over the questions that you had and felt that Mr. Spirit at the Department of Education should be able to help you with most of them. Teacher licensure (non-traditional or otherwise) is strictly handled by the Dept of Ed." On March 12, 2002, Mrs. Smarty, secretary for Mr. Spirit, Department of Education, told me to "hire an attorney after my interview with Mr. Spirit", where "he informed me that the third

university evaluation was proof that I couldn't teach". March 14, 2002 (#12 Email) Mrs. Fred states "It sounds like you were able to spend some time with Mr. Spirit. I've found him to be very helpful in the past on other issues". March 15, 2002 (#5-Email) Why did Mr. Spirit stated that "individual schools have the right to deny anyone/someone a degree/teaching certificate" when neither first university in '85 or second university in '93 did this? He said that this was your decision, Mr. Take & Mrs. Thought or state regulations." (#8-Email) Mr. Take stated "You will need to have Mr. Spirit respond to the questions since you are attempting to become licensed through the Non-Traditional Licensure Program." (#7-Email) Mrs. Fred stated "I think that the only route now is the non-traditional certification route." I called Mrs. Fore, Vice President of Student Affairs at the third university, to find out exactly what you would need to do to start the appeal procedures. I am sorry to tell you that she stated that you have already exhausted all of your appeal processes. The Dean of Education is Dr. Bliss. (#9-Email) My letter to Mr. Take stated "It has come to my attention that filed an appeal at the third university, can you tell me why I wasn't allowed to teach? March 18, 2002 (#5-Email) Mr. Take stated "I'm sorry you are having difficulty getting answers to your questions. I am not aware of any appeal process. You would have to contact the college or university about what their appeal process is for their decisions. March 21, 2002 (#?-Email) Mrs. Fred stated "Mr. Thought stated that he was really concerned about my situation, but how do we address?" (#2-Email) Mr. Fred states "I'll have to check with Mrs. Thought. He has been out the first of this week. I'll let you know as soon as I am able to catch up with him. June 3, 2002 (#16-Email) Mr. Take stated "Mr. Spirit will have to answer any questions regarding the Non-Traditional Licensure program. The third university will have to answer the questions you have for them. I can't answer these questions for you ." May 1, 2002 Dr. Petty wrote that I was "going through the Non-Traditional Program for Elementary teaching". Dr. Petty, Ph.D., also stated "that I have the necessary hours except for practice teaching." Why would he have written this note, if I weren't capable of teaching? As you can see from his written statement, Dr. Petty, Ph.D., felt that I could teach. Dr. David, Ph.D., his secretary is Mrs. Sue. By the way, Dr. David Ph.D., has all of the documentation to inforce my struggle to teach in Arkansas, should you need to see it. I recently applied for the Star Scholarship in Swift & was denied because the third university had not changed the "F's" on my transcript as ordered by US Federal Court in 1997 to "D's". Mrs. Point, Program Coordinator, State Teacher Assistance Resource (STAR) Program. She said she was sending me a copy for my records, 8.15.06. September 24, 2002, Mrs. Woo (whom is related to me) of Vast Public Schools allowed her staff to laugh at me for trying to teach. The ladies who were laughing were Mrs. Larry, Mrs. Wam, Mrs. Hoo, and Mrs. Soo. This was what they were saying about me, that I was "stupid", "brain injured", "laughing loudly that I had taken 247 college hours & wasn't this enough proof that I couldn't succeed/teach", etc. It didn't make my rehabilitation worth the effort, but shameful. This was the day before my anniversary of my accident in 1977. This was a tough day. October 26, 2002, Mrs. Ram said to me "I was no longer allowed on Smoke campus, since the Smoke school board meeting". October 28, 2002, Mrs. Sul Trauma Association was to & did contact Dr. Petty about behavior regarding exclusion, not allowing me to teach & saved document/email, but no word from her on this issue. December 4, 2002, Dr. Petty Smoke Public Schools, Superintendent, told me that (Teacher at Smoke) Mrs. Ram stated, "I can't teach".

Dr. Petty, Ph.D., feels that I can't teach either, since he stated, "Stop casing dream of teaching", However, he sent me to see Mr. Spirit, Dept of Education in June 2001 to obtain alternative certification & assisted me in writing a resume for teaching positions. Which I have in his handwriting from May 2001.

December 5, 2002, I called Mr. Sue, Principal of Jam. Elementary School, 12/5/02, hand written & told me that he had sent Dr. Petty, Ph.D., a positive letter of reference in 2001 about my teaching abilities. I, then asked Mrs. Sue to send a copy to Dr. Tye, Ph.D., to verify this fact, since Dr. Tye, Ph.D., needs proof that I can teach & suggested that my not working could be due to Mrs. Sue letter of reference. If a polygraph is needed, I'll submit. Mrs. Larry stated, secretary for Mr. Tally, Vast Superintendent, "Shaun you would have to tutor students, use computers, work in the kitchen, etc." Apparently she feels that I can't do this even after completing the workshop they held for this activity. January 31, 2003, Dr. Tye, Ph.D., stated that when he called Mrs. Sue of Jam about my teaching skills demonstrated at Task Elementary School, he replied "I can teach". On January 31, 2003, When I contacted the Smoke Public School (SPS) about posting Jumping Jack Advocacy Team (JJA) flyer superintendent, when I was treasurer, office referred me to Attorney but the elementary school at HPS said they would post flyer stated Mrs. Petty the wife of superintendent Dr. Petty whose secretary had just minutes earlier told me that any JJA materials/I would have to go through Attorney. Smoke is the community I live in, but why would a new superintendent be brought from a troubling school, was it another unethical move by the board, i.e., referring to the statement that Mr. Stone stated when I was forced to leave the room with Mrs. Ram regarding employment as a substitute? Mr. Stone stated "we don't need that teaching in our schools" as I left the room & I was told by a friend.

March 4, 2003, I received two certified letters sent from Vast Public Schools by Mr. Tally (Article Number 7099-3400-0002-5438-3270 sent February 28, 2003; then resent March 4, 2003 article number 7099-0002-5439-9462) for Employment Intent Form (EIF). At the bottom of this letter it states: "If you do plan to sign up to substitute, you will still need to complete forms in the bookkeeping office in August 2004." Therefore, I'm signed up to teach for fall 2003-spring 2004 with the needed credentials, which I've had since 1993. I returned both letters before the deadline of 3/7/03, because one of the copies I have has written statement/note in the lower right-handed corner "Copy/Mr. Tally has original", then the other copy of the EIF has nothing written in the lower right handed . This EIF was the first I received, since I started working at the schools in April 2000. Why haven't other schools done this? It should be noted that the Vast Public School (VPS) used my old address of Route 2 Box 32, Jazz, State 2222, which is the reason the first certified letter was delayed in getting to me, even after they worked me in February 2002 & knowing of my new address. By the way, Mrs. Woo took from September too March to answer my questions regarding the September event 2002, where she stated in a letter dated in September that she would response about the statements made by the administration at VPS. Her response came in March 2003 after I visited with Mrs. Xi March 10, 2003 about Mrs. Woo's late response to the statements from her co-workers on September 24th.

March 14, 2003, 9:45 a.m. on NBC Today, www.today.msnbc.com talked about a book that reinforces positivism over negativism. An optimistic attitude always benefits the progress or existence of everyone, even over illnesses.

On July 31, 2003, Sam is talking with the Smoke superintendent about me teaching this year. Sam's sister who was at the school board meeting also went with her to talk to him about me. Remember, she was the one that wrote the note/letter verifying that once you pass the substitute tests for one year you don't have to retake them every year in Swift, according to the elementary principal Mrs. Ram, Mrs. Sandy, etc. Mrs. Catch learned this September 17, 2002. According to Mr. Sun & in his years as superintendent, it has been that the classroom teacher who pick the substitute, on the substitute teacher's list, that they want to teach their students. This is the one reason /variable that has kept me from teaching or it could be one that is strongly reinforced, since the third university students (who teach all over Swift, etc.) were brainwashed to believe I was a danger, threat, hazard, etc., (brain disabled/brain damaged) to the students. I've all the following; when needed. Smoke' Request School Board Meeting 10.21.03; Large VPS Certified Letter 3/4/03 to my PO Box with this one it was either copy in Mr. Tally's office or the other; Dr. Petty wrote a short resume with Mrs. Jones contact person from work at Economic Center, etc., on back (his handwriting); VPS Certified Letter 3/3/03 sent to Rural Route Address, which is inside brown envelope, its white; other certified letter is in sealed letter from Vast Post Office, which can confirm that at least one was sent; Post office must keep on file for 2 years-February/March 2005; Green Slip 5438-3270.

September 17, 2003, Mr. Sky will call Mr. Sun around 2:30 pm 9.17.03 about teaching qualities, however Mr. Sky "complained why I used him solely as reference", when others like Rock Springs, Jonesville, Smoke, etc., & I told him that I used others, but since I had subbed for him more days he would have a better perspective of my teaching skills. Mr. Sky said "the reason
for not calling was long distance phone charge". Mr. Sun, when asked whether Mr. Sky had called responded "didn't know or hasn't heard of him". I visited with Mr. Sun about teaching at Smoke and he inquired why Mr. Sky of Vast had not called me back to substitute teach. Now, I had a reason to visit Mr. Sky & he told me that it was the cost of a long distance phone call that hindered his choice.

Others schools like Rock Springs, Smoke, Jonesville where fewer days were taught could not provide as good quality a reference. Mr. Sky had also been on my side when I applied for the Provisional Teacher Certification with the assistant of Superintendent Dr. Petty & Mrs. Ram, Elementary Principal at Smoke. Then on the 23rd of September after the Smoke Clubs meeting (check phone records) when I asked Mr. Sun whether Mr. Sky had called him like he assured me that he would on September 17 (2:30 p.m.) to acknowledge my teaching skills as he had done to Dr. Tye, Ph.D., Big Bend Co-Op, Mr. Sun replied that he "didn't know or hasn't heard of him".

September 23, 2003, I heard from Mrs. Catch that Mr. Big was on the Smoke School Board when Dr. Petty, Ph.D., was superintendent, made reference "that people with brain disabilities/cognitive challenges, shouldn't be around other students". The principal of Smoke Elementary Schools (Dr. Petty, Ph.D.) viewed me as "too slow" to teach, but allowed/encouraged me to apply for Big River Governor's Development Disabilities Commission as a teacher earlier the previous month. Mr. Sky of Task Elementary Schools didn't view my performance as slow, nor did his teachers in 2000 or 2001. Also, he has given me a good reference in 2003 to Dr. Tye, Ph.D., of the Extension Office in Big Bend.

Is this intentional/institutional discrimination? This allowed the state of Big River to deny me a teaching certificate & kept Mr. Tally, superintendent of Vast Schools, from filing my provisional teacher application in 2001. Is this an act to conspire me from teaching future adults, about the success of those with different abilities have? Isn't it strange how the Big River treats me?

November 25, 2003, Pastor Bird talked with me today 9/2/03 & Dr. Petty, Ph.D., never called him about me working at New Force Operation, Inc., like he said he was going to do. Pastor Bird stated "You have become ensnared by people who have mistreated you."

June 3, 2004 Dr. Petty, Ph.D., & Mrs. Ram allowed me to use them as teaching references. Dr. Petty, Ph.D., told me to have schools to call him in reference to my teaching skills. Everywhere I go, my competent abilities are neglected, could it be the harmful/negative stigma of Maplewood (Dr. Dwyer, Ph.D.)

The attorney who incorporated "Challenged Conquistadors, Inc.," as an educational organization, his wife-my former high school teacher, reinforced in court papers that I could not teach. Her name is Mrs. Sun and his name is Mr. Sun. He incorporated "Challenged Conquistadors, Inc., as a "Public-Benefit Corporation" with Sean Best as registered agent through the Swift Secretary of State, 6.2.95. My name was misspelled. His wife was my teacher in high school & one of the teachers I substituted for at the Schools that said I couldn't teach with/without accommodations.

Could he have held my organization against me? This experience wasn't pleasant.

July 23, 2003

To Whom It May Concern:

This letter of support is for Shaun Best of Smoke, Swift. Shaun was recruited in January of this year as a mentor, volunteer, and tutor for the developmentally disabled adults we work with at New Force Operations, a nonprofit sheltered workshop. Shaun has shown himself to be a role model for our clients, emulating to them the leadership qualities he possesses and encouraging them to develop their own. Just yesterday in our monthly support group, of which Shaun is a part, the very client whom he coached for our speech talent contest (and who won first place) was elected President of the client organization, which Shaun helped start!

A new Chapter of "Challenged Conquistadors" (CC) has been birthed here with Shaun's initiative. It is examples like the above that make us proud to be associated with Shaun Best. Our support and best wishes are offered him in all that he strives to accomplish. It is with admiration that we look at his track record in all that he has overcome. Not a quitter, Shaun will certainly continue to look for avenues in which he can make a difference in our society.

Mrs. Pace

New Force Operation
Rehab Coordinator

Additional proof that my recovery is seen as successful is the following nominations; Robert L. Moody Prize for Distinguished Initiatives in Brain Injury Research & Learning, Galveston, TX; 9.03 Joseph P. Kennedy, Jr., Foundation Public Policy Fellowship, Washington, DC, both nominations were by New Force Operation, where Rev. Bird, Ph.D., is a member of the board of directors. I can send these documents to you, if you should like them.

However; in court papers this lady (Mrs. Pace) denied my teaching abilities with children. Her & her supervisor stated "I couldn't teach children".

It should also be remembered that this experience was also an attempt to institutionalize myself, again. My mother wanted to institutionalize myself after my first brain injury in 1977.

Her brother tried to in 2004. New Force Operation, tried to confine my optimistic thinking of myself with the negative terms in the disability environment, i.e., disabled, handicapped, etc.

However, they started a chapter of the "Challenged Conquistadors, Inc.," at their location. Our boss, Mr. Hash, South Swift Development Center for Children & Families tried to convince Mrs. Sam that I was "low functioning", "low IQ", "barely functioning above those we would be taking care of as developmentally disabled individuals", in fact, "Mr. Hash had told Mrs. Sam that she could; get paid to take care of me", etc. We both worked had worked there at one time.

However, thankful to Ms. Sam my institutionalization did not happen. Mrs. Sam upon meeting me didn't believe what Mr. Hash had told her, we eventually became husband & wife. We thank Mr. Hash, a preacher, for our meeting, but she is still at a loss as why I was thought of as unable to function.

And most recently, I would like to share my journey to teach in Big Bend through the many turns in the road: First, I was recruited by the third university, the Foundations to promote awareness that brain injury recovery, through the "Challenged Conquistadors, Inc.", 6.2.95, is obtainable and ensure that the third university campus complied with the Americans with Disabilities Act of 1990. I survived a head injury in 1977, which made me useful for the grant.

Mrs. Fore, Mrs. George, Mrs. Roy, Dr. Ray, Ph.D. (I was on two of his Southern University teams, '95 and '96), Mr. Butt, etc., recommended that I enter the teaching field, since my research was reinforced by H. Gardner's book, The Unschooled Mind. Which a few years later, where the third university Professor Emeritus Dr. Tree, Ph.D., referenced my work to his book in an article she wrote for "A Journal of Faith". Then after completing my coursework at the third university, I had a 2.7 GPA, therefore I wasn't allowed to complete the practicum. However, I did merit the nomination by the third university School of Education for a teaching scholarship from the Swift Governor's Commission on People with Disabilities 3.13.97 written by Dr. Smart, Ph.D. Second, I tried the Non-Traditional Teacher Licensure Program using the JC City Public School, Mr. Can, as my avenue to teach, which was stamped by the Certification Division 6.14.01. Mr. Can told me to contact him after seeing Mr. Spirit on 6.19.01. He signed a note, as a reminder, indicating he wanted me to call him regarding Mr. Spirit's response. I called, but Mr. Can never responded. His, handwritten note on the bottom of his letter 6.25.01 indicates he desired me in the Non-Traditional program. Third, I tried attending the third university to finish my work, but they recommended (quicker-since I had a one college degree) contacting Mr. Take about completing my requirements through the Provisional Certification route, indicating it would be simpler that way, 7.19.01. I was successful in getting another public school to fill out this application, Vast Public Schools. Mr. Tally signed this form on 8.30.01. I was never allowed to start the program. Fourth, 2.26.02, Mr. Take in a letter to me wrote: "You need to complete the application & return it as quickly as possible to Mr. Spirit so he can complete the evaluation & get a response back to you.

Fifth, 3.11.02 email from Mrs. K. Camp Sixth, 5.1.02 Dr. Petty, Ph.D., of Smoke Public Schools wrote sketch of what I needed to tell the schools I applied at regarding the Non-Traditional Licensure Program. Dr. Petty, Ph.D. stated "Don't have certification but you'll go through Non-Traditional Program for Elementary". "I have the necessary hours except for practice teaching". The note is handwritten by Dr. Petty, Ph.D. Seventh, I received two Employment Intent Forms (3.5.03) from the Vast Public School by certified mail from Vast & the numbers are 8099-3400-0002-5438-3270 and 8099-3400-0002-5439-9462 and this one is signed by someone in the office indicating Mr. Tally has the original.

Eighth, I tried to attend the second university in May 2003, to participate in the "Master of Art in Teaching" (MAT) program, but again was unsuccessful "unable to act on your application at this time", stated Dr. Guess, Ph.D., Dean, School of Education. Who told me about this program, Mrs. Pace at New Force Operation? Ninth, from the Springs Rehabilitation, Neuropsychological Evaluation, 7.15.03, "there is no strong evidence that he would be unable to engage in the teaching profession". Tenth, I contacted Mrs. Pistol, who wrote a memo, 10.13.04: "Non Traditional Licensure (NTL) requested summary from court cases denying Mr. Best the opportunity to continue teacher certification at SU. NTL will have the summaries review by Swift Department of Education lawyer for a ruling on whether or not Mr. Best can enter the NTL Program." Eleventh, 8.12.05 & 11.21.05, I was involved with a new drug discovery for my condition, it wasn't used for my cognitive purposes until May 2005, Dr. Field, M.D., was one of the first to successfully utilize this medication. Dr. Field, M.D., wrote Dr. Ray, Ph.D., twice about this continuing/finishing my coursework and he is yet to respond to him (the last time was sent by certified mail through me). Twelfth, I spoke with the third university after US Senator contacted Dr. Ray, Ph.D./Dr. Scare, Ph.D., which got the third university desiring my application to complete my certificate. At the advice of friends, regarding my failed attempts at the third university '94-'99, they urged me to attend the fourth university. Thirteen, I've applied for admission and have been accepted to the fourth university, Dr. K. Post, Ph.D., is my advisor, where I am being allowed to complete my teacher education courses. Instead of me continually being denied, could Dr. Jack, Ph.D., find out, how I can succeed in my quest to teach & if the fourth university will be allowed to grant me a teaching certificate, should I be able to do the work? He hasn't answered this question, yet, however he tells me that the Non-Traditional Licensure Program is my best method to secure a teaching certificate.

As an individual, one may find it different for the state to treat me in an uncaring manner, because we saw how the third university treated me. Which is contrary to other universities, etc.

Watch and see how things unfold as another state employer continues to try my potential with cognitive challenges/head injuries.

February 21, 2006, I hit my head while pulling grass, again, when I fell out of the chair, which Mr. Space told me to use to reduce the chances of falling. The chair sunk down in the loose soil, causing me to fall out of the chair, several times.

March 2, 2006, Mr. Case (Safety Director), Mr. Space & I discussed buying a helmet for you when I was pulling grass, but Van said "my responsibility to get one". I called Dr. Field, MD., regarding a helmet. Mr. Space was sarcastic about me wearing a helmet, because of the image it would promote at the museum, since I would be in view of those attending museum. As of today, they've not bought knee pads to or for pulling grass, but they eventually did. The receipt will show the date bought.

March 7, 2006 Mr. Space wrote me a letter stating "Get all weeds out of Circle bed, spend more than 12 minutes on this. It's not too, hot yet, 30 minutes 1 hour, or until you get all weeds out. Thanks. Danny." I received the note: March 8, 2006. This is a dangerous activity, especially when balance is questionable when hot, especially with headaches.

March 29, 2006, I talked to Mr. Case about the two bosses-Ms. Fire & Mr. Space, conflicting. Also, in a written letter to Ms. Fire, I stated: "Wednesday, around 10-11 am, after being told by Mr. Space that my pulling grass looked well on grass section #2, which he said to leave some for job-security, I walked into the main house to start another job. The job was sweeping & mopping the back three rooms located on my duty list. As I finished sweeping one room Ms. Fire came in very agitated & stated "Shaun come with me". I knew I was in trouble.

I slowly walked behind her, like Mr. Space had said, trying to keep up with her. As we approached grass section #1 I hurried up such that I could see what she was pointing at. When I did, she spoke loudly in my right ear stating "Your job is pulling grass". She spoke loudly (after speaking with Ms. Fire, I said she yelled, she said differently) needless to say I missed Thursday work, because of the severe headache/pain that followed. I called Dr. Field & told him, Thursday, (about my head hurting as a result of her voice). The right side of the head still hurts with auditory problems in the right ear, Friday. Signed at Bottom: Shaun Best 3.31.06. I then gave this letter to Mr. Case, Safety Coordinator at the Museum; This is a dangerous activity (pulling grass) from the number of times I've fallen on my shoulders & hit head, etc., since I started in June '05. Ms. Fire knows that I've had several brain injuries, prior to working for the state. A member of the board of directors, Mrs. Button is a cousin, who knows that I've had several brain injuries & shouldn't do work that results in re-injuries.

March 31, 2006, I called Dr. Field, MD, about Ms. Fire yelling in her office at me, in regards to the negative statements, Ms. Fire stated of my performance & character. Ms. Fire & I talked behind closed doors. For the record, she "threatened to fire me", then she attacked my performance: "I was a liability & easy to replace";

"behavior is causing conflict between employees"; "poor job keeping the facility clean"; "most people only get three chances or they're fired, but she said, she was giving me a fourth chance to do the required assignments/tasks posted"; "accused me of acting like a two year old", "she didn't need me", "next time she raises her voice she'll try to be on other side of my head", etc. If you doubt that she said this, please call Dr. Field, MD, who called Ms. Fire 3.31.06 about the experimental/new medication (the side effects of Depakote) for my brain situation (Lamictal) I was taking, since I told him the same thing. The state has fired me before for being developmentally slow, South Swift Development Center for Children & Families. I took them to court & with the testimony of my wife, won. She told them what Mr. Hash stated about me: "I had a low IQ; was low functioning, could barely take care of himself, in fact, you could sign him up on Medicaid wavier & get paid to provide care for him (he didn't know he was talking to my future wife)" "you will be caring for him & another client"; etc. Could this be a reason Ms. Fire thought so lowly of me? I assume the headache she gave me made her mad. I was punished for this & fired. I also gave her a letter stating how her orders conflicted with my other boss, who was I to follow? Could this have also, made her mad? The number of times I fell on my head (4), back, etc., could have made her mad?

In fact, my physician has had to write the museum, because they feel that I quit my job. I'm battling for my unemployment compensation, because the state feels I quit. I had to have the surgery on my nose & tonsils for my health. He has written them to tell them I didn't quit and I was fired by Mrs. Fire in April. It is before a judge in Little Rock, who will weigh the evidence. Will I win or will I continue to loose? When you have employers like this medical interventions aren't successful. How many other employee's will be unable to work in society, because of such behavior?

April 6, 2006, Ms. Fire stated "creating dissension (quarreling) between the workers by behavior changes."

April 18, 2006, Ms. Fire asked, "If I wanted to resign"? I'll "allow one week you're your surgery."

April 19, 2006 after handing her my doctor's note, Ms. Fire stated "I'll need you here & I can't hold your job-I'll have to hire another". Why was this said, if I quit?

April 20, 2006, I called the Disability Rights Center about being fired by the Museum & Mrs. A. Razor who said to get policy handbook. I called & spoke with Mrs. Day at the museum.

May 15, 2006, Ms. Fire stated that the "state of Arkansas had run out of funds for my position," when I returned to work as scheduled, but there was another person hired for the job that I had been doing. Why was this statement made by Ms. Fire, if I didn't give notice as the State Workforce Letter dated (5.17.06) state, however on 4.18.06 Ms. Fire stated she "would allow one week for surgery", and therefore I did give her notice. She did offer to let me work one hour a day, pulling grass, after my surgery. I told her that my health is more important or I would not risk falling after the surgery and I needed time to prepare for college at the fourth university.

Why would the state endanger my health with work like pulling grass, where I had fallen many times on my head/shoulders/back? It is incredible that the state wanted to endanger my health, but this happens in Swift. These are a few experiences by the state of Swift. Last but not least, are some recent statements that were made by my other employers, i.e., store, Mrs. Paula, stated "Shaun you need to accept that your brain is disabled & you can not teach". Ask my wife how I took the information. "Too slow, threats, environmental risk factors-noise, raciest, denied breaks, threats to fire, some wanted me to fight them, etc., another employer. He is so slow, can't he think faster/better, yet, another employer, etc. Those statements from the schools are teachers/administrators/attorneys, etc., who have known me from high school or grew up with me-in our community, relatives, etc.

As you can see, even with the facts as such, I still did not win or was allowed to teach. I hope that this adventure, story can enhance others belief in themselves, after traumatic brain challenges, even when the deck is stacked against them, because they can succeed? Nature conditions us to succeed; disabilities /challenges enhance our natural potential. Thank you for your time & may others learn from our tenacity.

Believe it or not I was rehabilitated by 1978 & yet this treatment continues. It really matters, when you have a head challenge/injury. You can naturally recover, as I did, but society may never view you as competent after an injury /challenge? This is a loss for our society, because many brain challenged individuals stay at home, because of the outdated perception of our limited recovery. If there were more of us seen positively, this could benefit our entire world.

Thank you for this opportunity. Have A Best Day the Optimistic Way: Positivism!!

My bottom goal is to act as an agent of positive change, hopefully we can work together for everyone's best potential? What is so troublesome is the amount of time that I was intentionally blocked from the education of future adults, when a needed positive role model for those dealing with cognitive challenges was needed. However, it is better late than never.

I would like to share the good news and hope these stories can be utilized in a productive manner.

To end on my darling wife, ended up trying to kill me in 2014 and the Arkansas state police will not arrest her for attempted murder

of a protected individual by the National Silver Alert Program, she
was my advocate.

Have A Optimistic Day the Best Way: Positivism!! God is the
greatest, the end!

Mr. Shaun Best, Protector of the Natural State
Challenged Conquistadors, Inc.
1110 Pine Circle
Smackover, AR 71762